Contents

Introduction

Those who have lost a loved one have a universal need for comfort. Our grandmother Helen Margaret Beasley Bellm passed away in 1985. After her death, family members donated her dresses to a local church. Her oldest grandson and our cousin, Jim Rives, learned of the donation and wanted the dresses back. He needed something tangible to help him remember our grandmother and thought the dresses could be made into a quilt. He began his quest to hunt them down. Luckily, the search was brief and Jim was able to find them. Not knowing anyone who quilted, he held onto them for 14 years. At a family reunion, he learned about our interest in quilting and asked if we would consider making a quilt for him. We jumped at the chance.

Jim, however, had one stipulation before he turned over those dresses to our rotary cutters: we had to base the quilt on a floral pattern. Grandma had a green thumb, and her pride and joy was her garden. Visitors at Grandma's house were always treated to a tour of her flower beds. She had a right to be proud. Her backyard was the envy of everyone in town.

We were thrilled to take on the project and felt that Grandma was watching over us the entire time. As payment, Jim let us keep the leftover fabric to make Granny quilts of our own. These quilts are special and truly comforting.

Grandma's dresses were old, well worn, and of questionable fiber content. We knew this quilt would have to be handled differently than a quilt made with newer, 100%-cotton fabric. We weren't sure where to begin. We looked for books on the subject, but found none. Without a guide, we had to start from scratch and learn many different techniques to allow us to work with these old clothes. We share with you what we found out about working with many types of clothing fabrics in "Working with Recycled Garment Fabrics" on page 10.

Of course, all the quilt projects in this book can be made with new fabric. They can also be made from different garment fabrics than what we selected for our quilts. Look for the "What If . . ." box that follows each project for some ideas on how to change the look of the original quilt to suit your own memories.

Come See My Garden *made by Ann Frischkorn and owned by Jim and Eileen Rives. Photo by Don Sandrin, Vantevision Photography. Modeled by Jax the cat, who owns Don and Amy Sandrin.*

Working with Recycled Garment Fabrics

We knew there had to be many people like us who were looking for answers on how to use clothing in quilts, and we felt it was our destiny to help those people find the answers they were seeking. This chapter will cover how to use many types of garment fabrics in your quiltmaking. Each section will give general guidelines on how to prepare and sew with a specific fabric.

In general, when salvaging fabrics from garments, remove buttons (save them for embellishments) and zippers. Cut off waistbands, collars, cuffs, plackets, linings, and seam bindings and discard. Remove the thread from hems and pleats.

VINTAGE COTTON AND POLYESTER-COTTON BLENDS

- Wash and dry all fabric on the gentle cycle and press out any wrinkles.

- If the fabric is worn, thin, or lacking in body, line it with a lightweight fusible interfacing, following the manufacturer's instructions.

- Some fabrics that contain polyester will burn easily with a hot iron. Unless you're certain that the fiber content is 100% cotton, it's best to iron a small piece first or, when in doubt, start with a lower setting.

- Hand or machine piece, using a ¼" seam allowance.

- Use 100% cotton for the quilt backing.

- Use your favorite batting.

- Hand baste or pin baste the quilt layers together as you normally would before quilting.

- Hand or machine quilt.

- For the binding, use 100% cotton in a color that complements the quilt.

FLANNEL

- Flannel shrinks about 4% to 7% during laundering, which is nice to know when purchasing new flannel, but not too important if old, worn clothing is used. If new flannel has been purchased to supplement the worn clothing, wash it at least two times in hot water, drying after each washing in a hot dryer.

- If your flannels are of varying thicknesses, go ahead and use them anyway; the thickness will sink into the batting once the fabric is quilted and you won't see the difference.

- Spray the flannel with spray sizing or starch before rotary cutting. Because flannel tends to be soft and floppy, the spray sizing or starch will help the flannel hold its shape, which makes piecing a lot less frustrating.

- Use a rotary cutter to cut flannel; don't use scissors.

- Flannel has a lower thread count than most cotton fabrics, causing it to stretch easily during handling. To avoid this problem, use a lot of pins. Many quilters prefer to use a walking foot to keep the layers from shifting.

- The lower thread count can also cause raveling. To allow for any fraying that might occur, use ½" seam allowances. In this book, ½" seam allowances have been included in cutting dimensions for projects that use flannel fabrics. If you want to take the time, use a zigzag stitch to finish the fabric edges.

- Use 100%-cotton thread in the top and in the bobbin when piecing.

- When pressing flannel blocks, use a hot, dry iron. Don't use steam; it will relax the weave, possibly distorting the blocks. Some quilters swear by pressing their flannel seams open. This is a matter of personal preference.

- Flannel produces a lot of lint. Clean your sewing machine frequently.

- Flannel will dull a needle quickly, so change it often.

- Because flannel stretches so much, when determining the size of your borders, be sure to use the measurement of what the quilt length and width *should* be and not what it actually measures.

- Use a 100%-cotton fabric (flannel or otherwise) for the quilt backing.

- Batting is a matter of preference. A lightweight cotton batting will work nicely. If you want a lightweight quilt, omit the batting and use flannel for the backing.

- When basting the layers together, use tons of safety pins.

- Flannel is hard to needle, so hand quilting is usually not recommended for flannel quilts, unless the big-stitch method is used. For the big-stitch method, use No. 8 pearl cotton and a large needle to take ¼"-long stitches. This technique will give a folk-art quality, which looks great on flannel.

- When machine quilting, you might want to use a longer stitch length so that the stitches lie flatter on the surface. Quilt with 40-weight, 100%-cotton thread and a 90/14 needle.

- Simple, straight-line quilting patterns, using the walking foot, work best. A pattern with gentle curves works also.

- For the binding, use flannel, homespun, broadcloth, or any 100%-cotton in a color that complements the quilt. If you use flannel, cut the binding ¼" wider than usual to allow for the ½" seam.

- Always wash the quilt as soon as possible after finishing it to remove the starch, which could eventually destroy the fibers in the fabric and attract bugs.

MEN'S TIE FABRICS

❖ Before you can use men's ties, they must be taken apart and washed. Remove the stitching on the back of the ties and open them up. Remove the batting from each one and discard it. Place the ties in a mesh laundry bag designed for lingerie. Wash the fabrics in cold water with a mild soap. Keep the ties in the lingerie bag and dry them in the dryer on a medium setting. Press out any wrinkles with a dry iron on a low setting, pressing from the wrong side. If there are any stubborn wrinkles, lightly spray them with water and they should come out when pressed. If that doesn't work, mix a teaspoon of vinegar with a pint of water in a spray bottle. Lightly spray the solution onto the wrinkle, and then press. Each tie will yield approximately ⅛ yard of fabric.

❖ Ties tend to be slippery and hard to work with. To make them more manageable and to prevent raveling, apply a lightweight fusible interfacing to the wrong side of the tie fabric, following the manufacturer's instructions. This step is optional but recommended.

❖ If you interface the ties, use a ¼" seam allowance when piecing. If you opt not to interface the ties, use a ½" seam allowance, because the fabrics tend to ravel.

❖ Use a slightly shorter stitch length of about 15 stitches to the inch instead of the usual 12.

❖ Press seam allowances open to reduce bulk.

❖ Use 100% cotton for the quilt backing.

❖ Use your favorite batting.

❖ Thread baste or pin baste the layers together. If pin basting, do not use any needles or pins that are dull or blunt because they might damage the silky fabrics that ties are usually made of.

❖ Quilting will not show up very well on busy tie patterns. Simple quilting, such as quilting in the ditch or straight-line quilting, is your best bet.

❖ To bind the quilt, use 100% cotton or silk in a color that complements the quilt.

SILKY FABRICS

❧ Silk and silky fabrics can be difficult to work with, because they fray terribly and are slippery. To eliminate these problems, follow the manufacturer's instructions to apply a very lightweight fusible interfacing to the wrong side of the fabrics.

❧ Don't pull on any loose threads; doing so could cause a snag that runs the entire length of the fabric. Gently cut away loose threads with scissors.

❧ Work with clean hands and avoid applying hand lotion right before you work with silky fabrics to avoid staining them. Spray starch will also stain these fabrics and is not recommended.

❧ Dry cleaning is the preferred method for cleaning quilts that are made entirely of silk fabrics. If you're using 100%-cotton and silk fabrics in the same quilt, the quilt can be washed if you prewash the silk fabric before you apply the interfacing. Quilts made from synthetic silky fabrics can also be washed. Wash them on a gentle cycle, and do not use fabric softener in the washer or dryer because it can leave "oily" spots on the fabric.

❧ When working with two different fabrics in one quilt, such as cotton and silk, always set the iron for the most delicate fabric.

❧ Use 100% cotton as a backing for a silk quilt. If you can find it, a silk-cotton mix also works nicely.

❧ Use a good-quality, thin cotton batting.

❧ Hand baste or pin baste the layers together. If you pin baste, do not use any needles or pins that are dull or blunt because they could damage the fabric.

❧ Quilt by hand or machine, using silk thread for silk fabrics and polyester thread for synthetic fabrics. If quilting by hand, it's OK to use a hoop or frame with silky fabrics, but be careful that the hoop hardware does not snag the fabric.

❧ For the binding, use either a fabric with a fiber content that matches your silky fabrics or 100% cotton in a color that complements the quilt.

WOOL

❖ Before wool-garment fabric or newly purchased wool can be used for the project on page 71, the wool must be felted. Felting causes the fibers to shrink and bind together, creating a denser and slightly darker fabric that will not ravel. Wool knits should be avoided, because they stretch and pucker. To felt wool, remove any selvage edges. Wash the fabric in hot water with mild detergent and rinse with cold water. If you're washing more than one fabric, wash like colors together. Check the washing machine often during each load. If there are loose fibers on the surface, remove them to prevent clogging the drain. Dry the fabric in the dryer on the hottest setting. Clean the lint tray several times during each cycle. When the wool is dry, check it to see if the edges ravel. If they do, repeat the wash and dry cycles until there is no raveling.

❖ Felted wool is great for appliqué, because it doesn't ravel, so no turn-under allowance is required. Appliqué the pieces in place by machine or hand with a blanket stitch.

❖ Felted wool quilts can be washed in the machine using a mild detergent, but they take a very long time to dry. Dry cleaning works best.

❖ Use a standard ¼" seam allowance; or omit the seam allowance, butt the edges of the pieces to-gether, and join them with a decorative or zigzag stitch.

❖ Wool will dull your needle quickly, so change the needle more often than you usually would and clean the lint out of your machine frequently.

❖ A flannel or 100%-cotton backing will comple-ment a wool quilt wonderfully.

❖ A thin, lightweight batting is sufficient for wool quilts. Some quilters opt for no batting at all.

❖ Hand baste or pin baste the layers together.

❖ Quilt by hand or machine. If quilting by hand, use two or three strands of embroidery floss or a single strand of pearl cotton. These threads are thicker and will lie very nicely on top of the wool fibers. Felted wool has a lot of loft; therefore, machine quilting should show up nicely. It is difficult to mark wool for quilting, so a free-motion design is recommended.

❖ Tying is another method used to secure the lay-ers of a wool quilt. Use No. 5 pearl cotton thread with a chenille needle. Place square knots about 4" apart.

❖ To bind the quilt, use 100% cotton in a color that complements the quilt.

❖ Wool is very sturdy and can withstand heavy embellishments. Beading looks especially nice on wool. When embroidering on wool, use a heavy-weight thread so the thread doesn't sink down into the wool fibers.

Paper-Piecing Instructions

Several of the quilts in this book have blocks that are paper pieced. This technique is great for accurately piecing points and small shapes. To paper piece blocks, follow these steps.

1. Using a lightweight paper that's easy to see through, such as tracing paper, make a copy of the pattern for each block you're going to sew. Martingale & Company sells foundation-piecing paper for this purpose, and you should be able to find it at any quilt shop. It can be used in any copy machine or laser printer.

2. Cut the fabric pieces needed for each area of the pattern as instructed for the project. Even though these pieces are precut, it's a good idea to double-check to make sure the fabric pieces are large enough to cover the entire area with enough excess fabric for seam allowances. It's better to have a fabric piece that's too large rather than too small.

3. Place the wrong side of the fabric piece for area 1 against the unprinted side of area 1 on the paper pattern. Hold the pattern up to a light source to make sure all edges of the area are covered by the fabric and that there is at least ¼" extra around all edges.

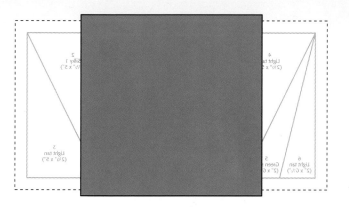

4. With right sides together, take the fabric for area 2 and place it over piece 1. Make sure the fabric extends beyond the stitching lines (solid lines) on all sides. Holding the fabric in place, flip the paper over to the printed side and stitch on the solid line between areas 1 and 2, using about 15 stitches per inch. Stitch all the way to the cutting lines (dashed lines). Trim the seam allowance to ¼".

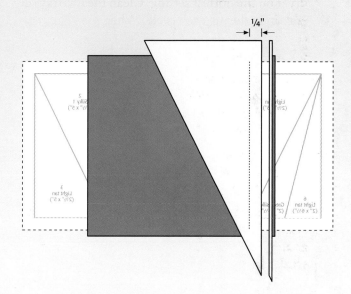

5. Open fabric piece 2 so that it covers area 2. Make sure the fabric extends at least ¼" over the stitching line that separates areas 2 and 3. Press the piece in place.

6. Working in numerical order, continue the process in the same manner until all pieces are sewn on.

7. Stitch all the way around the outside edge of the unit between the stitching line and the cutting line. This will hold the edges in place nicely.

8. Using a ruler and a rotary cutter, trim along the cutting line all the way around the unit.

9. Do not remove the paper until the quilt top is completed or until instructed. When the paper is ready to be removed, tear gently along the stitching lines. Tweezers are a great tool for removing the paper.

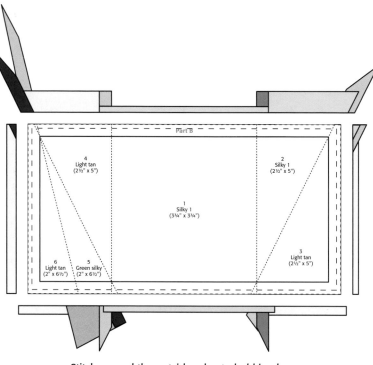

Stitch around the outside edge to hold in place.
Trim along the cutting line.

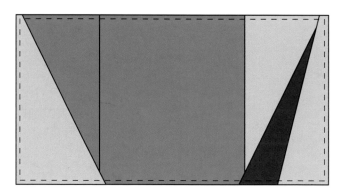

Completed unit from right side

Finishing Your Quilt

Now that your quilt top is done, it's time to quilt it. Here are some basic instructions that will get you on your way!

MARKING THE QUILTING DESIGN ON THE QUILT TOP

If the quilt needs to be marked with a quilting pattern, mark it before the layers are basted together. Marking a pattern is not necessary if the quilt will be stitched in the ditch, outline quilted, stipple quilted, or free-motion quilted with any design.

Test the marking tool on a piece of scrap fabric to make sure the marks can be removed easily. Masking tape can be used to mark straight-line quilting. Do not leave the tape on the fabric overnight, because it might leave a sticky residue.

LAYERING AND BASTING THE QUILT

Before you can quilt your top, it must be layered with batting and backing, and basted together.

1. To layer and baste the quilt, place the backing fabric, right side down, on a flat surface, such as a table or a hard floor. Tape the fabric to the surface on all four sides. Masking tape works best.

2. Working around the quilt, lift up one section of tape at a time and gently pull and straighten out the fabric. The fabric should be smooth and fairly taut.

3. Center the batting on top of the backing fabric and smooth it out with your hands.

4. Place the quilt top, right side up, over the batting. Center the top and smooth out any wrinkles with your hands.

5. If you're machine quilting, pin baste with safety pins, starting in the center and working outward. If

you're hand quilting, thread baste, starting in the center and working out in all four directions.

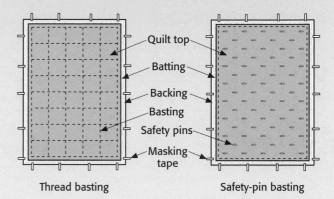

Thread basting   Safety-pin basting

MACHINE QUILTING

For straight-line quilting, a walking foot will produce the best results. The walking foot helps feed all three quilt layers through the machine evenly, thus avoiding shifting and puckering. If you're free-motion quilting, you'll need a darning foot, and the feed dogs should be dropped. With free-motion quilting, the fabric can be guided in any direction necessary without turning the quilt.

Start quilting in the center of the quilt and work your way toward the outside edges. If the fabric print is very busy, don't waste time with elaborate designs because they won't show up very well. Elaborate designs show up best on plain fabrics.

HAND QUILTING

Hand quilting requires quilting needles, quilting thread, and a thimble. Most quilters support their quilts in a frame or hoop, although some hand quilters quilt without any support at all.

1. Thread the quilting needle with an 18" length of quilting thread, knotting one end. Bring the needle down through the top layer only, about an inch from where you will start quilting. Bring the needle back up at the point where you want to start. Give a gentle tug to pop the knot through the top layer and into the batting, locking the knot in place.

2. Take small, evenly spaced stitches through all three quilt layers. Rock the needle in an up-and-down motion, gathering three to four stitches on the needle. Make sure stitches are even on the front and back of the quilt. Put your nonquilting hand underneath the layers so you can feel the needle coming through the back of the quilt.

3. To finish, make a small knot close to your last stitch and then backstitch, taking the thread a needle's length through the batting. Gently tug the thread until the knot pops through the top layer and into the batting. Snip the thread at the surface of the quilt.

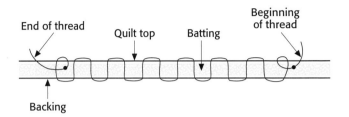

End of thread   Quilt top   Batting   Beginning of thread

Backing

BINDING THE QUILT

1. Cut the binding strips as indicated in the quilt instructions.

2. Stitch the strips together as shown to make one long strip. A diagonal seam is preferred because it is less visible and less bulky. Trim ¼" from the stitching line and press the seams open.

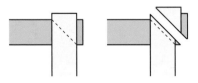

3. Trim one end of the strip at a 45° angle. Press the angled end under ¼". Press the strip in half lengthwise, wrong sides together.

4. Place the angled, folded-under end of the strip about one quarter of the way down on the right-hand side of the quilt. Stitch the binding to the quilt top, using a ¼" seam allowance and leaving the first 8" of the binding unstitched. Stitch toward the corner of the quilt, stopping ¼" from the edge. Backstitch one or two stitches. Clip your thread.

5. Turn the quilt to stitch down the next side. Fold the binding strip up, away from the quilt, forming a 45°-angle fold at the corner and keeping the raw edges aligned.

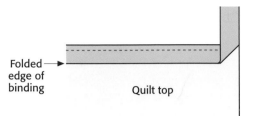

Folded edge of binding   Quilt top

6. Holding the fold in place, bring the strip back down onto itself, still keeping the raw edges aligned. Sew from the top of the fold, backstitching the first few stitches and continuing all the way down to ¼" from the next corner. Repeat the folding and stitching process at each corner.

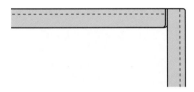

7. Stop stitching about 3" to 4" from the starting point of the binding. Measure the end of the binding so it overlaps the beginning by 1" to 2". Cut away the excess, trimming at a 45° angle. Slip the end of the binding inside the beginning, and finish sewing, backstitching at the end.

8. Trim the backing and batting even with the edge of the quilt top.

9. Fold the binding over the edge of the quilt to the back, just covering the edge of the machine stitching; blindstitch the binding in place. At each corner, a miter will form. Blindstitch these miters in place also.

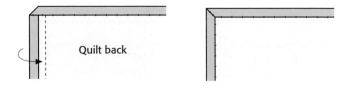

Quilt back

18

LABELS

Last, but not least, a label should be added to the back of the quilt. Labels should include the name of the maker, city and state, and year the quilt was made. Other information you may want to include: the recipient of the quilt; the occasion for which the quilt was made (wedding, anniversary, birth of baby, etc.); what pattern was used; the name of the quilt; how the quilt was made (quilted, pieced, or appliquéd by hand or machine); size of the quilt (comes in handy for entering shows or contests so you don't have to measure again); and washing instructions (especially nice when the quilt is given as a gift). If the quilt has a story behind it, include that as well.

We usually make our labels on plain muslin and then hand stitch them to the back of our quilts.

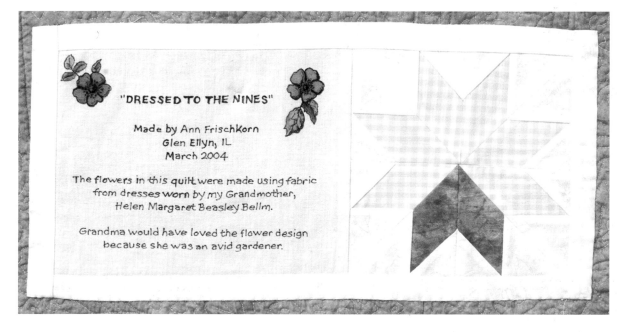

Dressed to the Nines

Pieced and quilted by Ann Frischkorn.

Finished quilt: 50¾" x 50¾" ❧ **Finished block:** 10" x 10"

This Carolina Lily quilt was re-created from an antique quilt called "Peony," which was made in 1863 by Catharine Graves Brockway of Vermont. The flowers in my quilt were made using fabric from my late grandmother's dresses. Words cannot describe how special and comforting this quilt is to me. As an added touch, I stitched buttons from Grandma's dresses to the center of each flower.

—Ann

MATERIALS

Yardage is based on 42"-wide fabric unless otherwise noted.

3 yards of light beige fabric for pieced block backgrounds, unpieced blocks, and binding

¼ yard *each* of 9 assorted fabrics for pieced block flowers

1½ yards of medium beige fabric for setting triangles and borders

1⅜ yards of green fabric for leaves, stems, and vine

3½ yards of fabric for backing

57" x 57" piece of batting

Papers for foundation piecing

Freezer paper

Water-soluble glue stick

Water- or air-soluble marker

Muslin or light-colored fabric, cut to desired size, for a quilt label

3 *each* of 9 different-colored buttons to match the assorted fabrics for block flowers (27 total)

CUTTING

All measurements include ¼" seam allowances.

From *each* of the 9 assorted fabrics, cut:

- 2 strips, 1¾" x 42"

From the green fabric, cut:

- 4 strips, 1¾" x 42"
- 1 strip, 15" x 42"; crosscut into 2 squares, 15" x 15"
- 3 strips, ¾" x 42"; crosscut into 9 rectangles, ¾" x 11"

From the light beige fabric, cut:

- 20 strips, 2¼" x 42"
- 12 strips, 2" x 42"
- 2 strips, 10½" x 42"; crosscut into 4 squares, 10½" x 10½". From the leftover strip, cut 4 squares, 5½" x 5½".
- 1 strip, 5½" x 42"; crosscut into 5 squares, 5½" x 5½"

From the medium beige fabric, cut:

- 1 strip, 15½" x 42"; crosscut into 2 squares, 15½" x 15½". Cut each square twice diagonally to yield 8 side setting triangles.
- 1 strip, 8" x 42"; crosscut into 2 squares, 8" x 8". Cut each square once diagonally to yield 4 corner setting triangles.
- 5 strips, 4½" x 42"

21

MAKING THE BLOCKS

1. Cut each of the assorted 1¾"-wide strips into 18 diamonds with a base of 2½" as shown. These will be used for section 1 of the paper-piecing units.

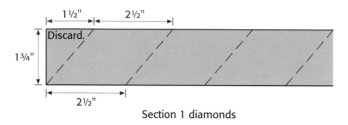

Section 1 diamonds

2. Repeat step 1 with the green 1¾"-wide strips to cut 54 diamonds.

3. Cut the light beige 2"-wide strips into 216 triangles with a base of 4" as shown. These will be used for section 2 of the paper-piecing units.

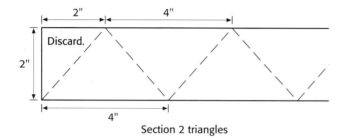

Section 2 triangles

4. Cut 14 of the light beige 2¼"-wide strips into 216 triangles with a base of 4½" as shown. These will be used for section 3 of the paper-piecing units.

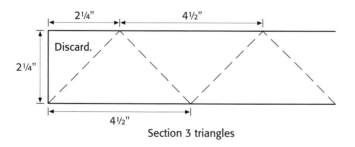

Section 3 triangles

5. Refer to "Paper-Piecing Instructions" on pages 15 and 16 to make 108 patterns *each* of units A and B.

6. Place a diamond cut from one flower fabric on section 1 of nine A units and nine B units. Place a green diamond on section 1 of three A units and three B units. Paper piece these units, using the appropriate triangles cut in steps 3 and 4 for sections 2 and 3.

> *I found it helpful to mark a green X on section 1 of three A and three B units so I wouldn't forget to make them green.*

7. Sew a green A unit to a green B unit. Make three. Sew each of the remaining A units to a B unit. Make nine. Sew the A and B pairs together in the order shown to make the three flower heads. Press all seams open to avoid bulk in the center of the block. Take care to place the green sections in the correct position. Do not remove the paper foundations yet.

> *Pin two pieces together and baste the seam. If the seams match up perfectly, stitch over the basting stitches with a normal stitch length. If they don't match up, you can easily rip out the basting and adjust the pieces.*

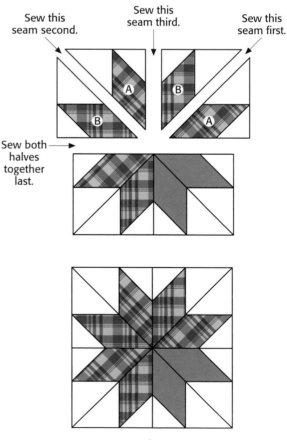

Make 3.

8. Sew the three flower heads and one light beige 5½" square together as shown. Remove the paper.

9. Repeat steps 6–8 to make a total of nine pieced squares.

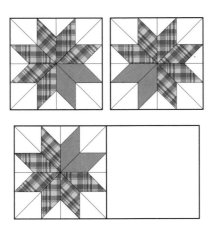

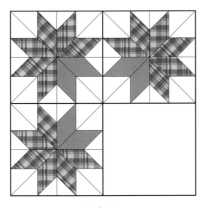

Make 9.

APPLIQUÉING THE STEMS

1. Place the pieced squares on point so the beige 5½" square is on the bottom. To mark the placement of the center stem, use a sharp pencil or draw a thin line from the bottom of the center flower to the bottom of the square.

2. To make the bias strips needed for the side stems, lay one of the green 15" squares on your cutting mat. Place the 45° line of your rotary-cutting ruler along one edge and make a cut. Measuring from this cut, cut ¾"-wide strips. You will need 18 pieces that are 11" long. Trim longer strips to the length needed and piece shorter strips together as necessary to achieve the required length. Cut one

end of each strip at a 90° angle, rather than on the diagonal.

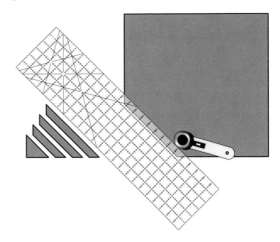

3. Press the bias strips in thirds, wrong sides together.

4. On the 90°-angle end of the strip, fold under the sides to make a point as shown. This will allow the stem to butt up nicely against the leaves on the flower. If this is too bulky, trim away some of the fabric from underneath the stems.

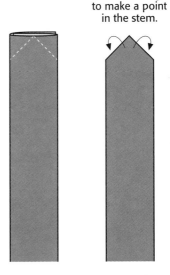

Fold under edges to make a point in the stem.

5. Pin the side stems in place on each pieced square as shown on page 24. The pointed ends should butt up nicely against the leaves on the side flowers; the bottoms of the stems should end at the marked line you drew in step 1. Trim away any excess length from the bottom of the stem. The bottoms of the two stems can meet, but they do not need to. Appliqué the stems in place by hand

or machine, using a blind hem stitch and matching green thread.

6. To make the center stems, fold the green ¾" x 11" rectangles in thirds, wrong sides together. Press. Fold under the sides of one end of the strip as you did in step 4 for the bias stems.

7. Pin each stem in place on the drawn line you marked in step 1. Trim away any excess length from the bottom of the stem. Appliqué the stems in place by hand or machine, using a blind hem stitch and matching green thread.

APPLIQUÉING THE LEAVES

1. Trace the flower leaf pattern on page 26 onto the dull side of the freezer paper 19 times. Cut out each template on the line. Iron the freezer-paper templates, shiny side down, onto the wrong side of the green fabric, leaving about ½" of space between each template. Cut out each fabric shape so it is approximately ¼" larger than the template.

2. Apply the water-soluble glue stick to the edge of the templates. Turn the excess fabric over so it sticks to the templates. If your edges aren't quite smooth enough, use a toothpick or stiletto to adjust and smooth the fabric while the glue is still wet.

3. Pin the leaves to the squares as desired and appliqué them in place by hand or machine, using a blind hem stitch and matching green thread.

4. Cut away the fabric behind the appliquéd leaves, leaving a ¼" seam allowance. Remove the

freezer-paper shapes: Dampen the paper so it will lift out easier by laying a damp cloth over the back of the block for a few minutes. The dampness will soften the glue and the paper should lift right out.

ASSEMBLING THE QUILT

1. Arrange the blocks and side setting triangles into five diagonal rows as shown.

2. Sew the blocks and triangles in each row together. Press all the seams in one row in the same direction, alternating the pressing direction from row to row.

3. Sew a corner triangle to each corner of the quilt top.

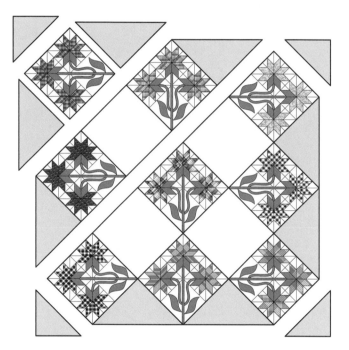

4. Because the setting triangles were cut a little larger than needed, you will need to trim off the excess ¼" from the block points.

5. Stitch two medium beige 4½" x 42" strips together end to end. Measure the width of the quilt top through the center and trim the pieced strip to this measurement. Make two. Sew the strips to the top and bottom of the quilt top. Press the seam allowances toward the borders.

6. Measure the length of the quilt top through the center, including the just-added borders. Stitch the pieces that you cut off of the top and bottom borders to the remaining 4½" x 42" strips. Trim

the pieced strips to the length measured, trimming from the end farthest from the seam so it is not too close to the edge. Sew the strips to the sides of the quilt top. Press the seam allowances toward the borders.

Quilt assembly

APPLIQUÉING THE BORDER

1. Refer to step 2 of "Appliquéing the Stems" to cut ¾"-wide bias strips from the remaining green 15" square. Stitch the strips together end to end until a length of approximately 210" is achieved. Press the pieced strip in thirds, wrong sides together.

2. Draw a placement line for the vine on the border with a water- or air-soluble marker.

3. Pin the vine to the border and appliqué it in place by hand or machine, using a blind hem stitch and matching green thread.

4. Trace the border leaf/flower bud pattern on page 26 onto the dull side of freezer paper 76 times. Cut out each template on the line. Iron 64 freezer-paper templates, shiny side down, onto the wrong side of the remaining green fabric, leaving about ½" of space between each template. Iron the remaining 12 templates to the wrong side of leftover flower fabrics. Cut out each fabric shape so it is approximately ¼" larger than the template.

5. Apply the water-soluble glue stick to the edge of the templates. Turn the excess fabric over so it sticks to the templates. If your edges aren't quite smooth enough, use a toothpick or stiletto to adjust and smooth the fabric while the glue is still wet.

6. Refer to the photo on page 20 to pin the buds and leaves to the vine. Appliqué the shapes in place by hand or machine, using a blind hem stitch and matching thread.

7. Remove the freezer-paper templates from the border in the same manner you removed the freezer-paper templates from the blocks.

FINISHING THE QUILT

Refer to "Finishing Your Quilt" on pages 17–19 for detailed information on finishing techniques.

1. Cut the quilt backing so that it is approximately 6" longer and 6" wider than the quilt top.

2. Layer the quilt top, batting, and backing; baste the layers together.

3. Hand or machine quilt as desired. This quilt was trapunto quilted by machine in the blank squares and setting triangles. Stipple quilting was used behind the Carolina lilies. The flower petals were quilted ¼" in from the edge. Veins were quilted into all of the leaves, using a slightly contrasting green thread.

4. Bind the quilt with the remaining light beige 2¼"-wide strips.

5. Label the quilt and relive fond memories of your loved one whenever you look at it.

What If . . .

- you saved your children's 100%-cotton clothing from the day they were born and made them a quilt as a gift for their high school or college graduation, or as a wedding gift?

- you made the flowers from silks or batiks?

- the flowers were white or a light color and the background was dark?

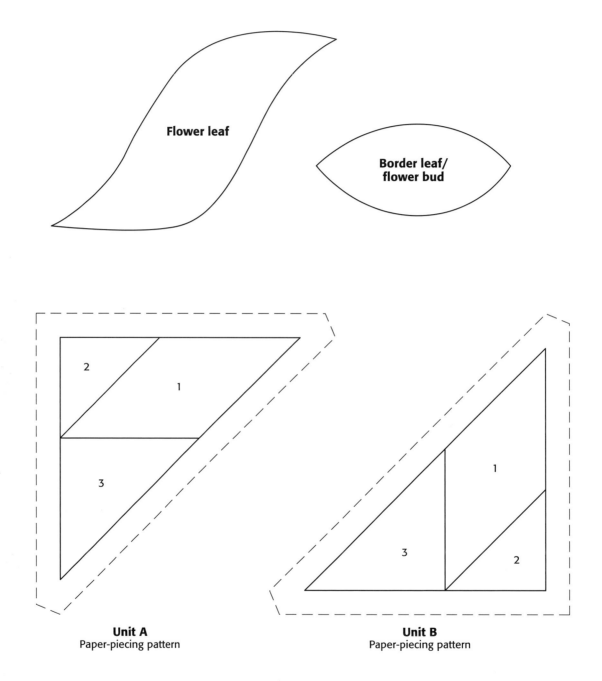

Flower leaf

**Border leaf/
flower bud**

Unit A
Paper-piecing pattern

Unit B
Paper-piecing pattern

Bellm Tree of Life

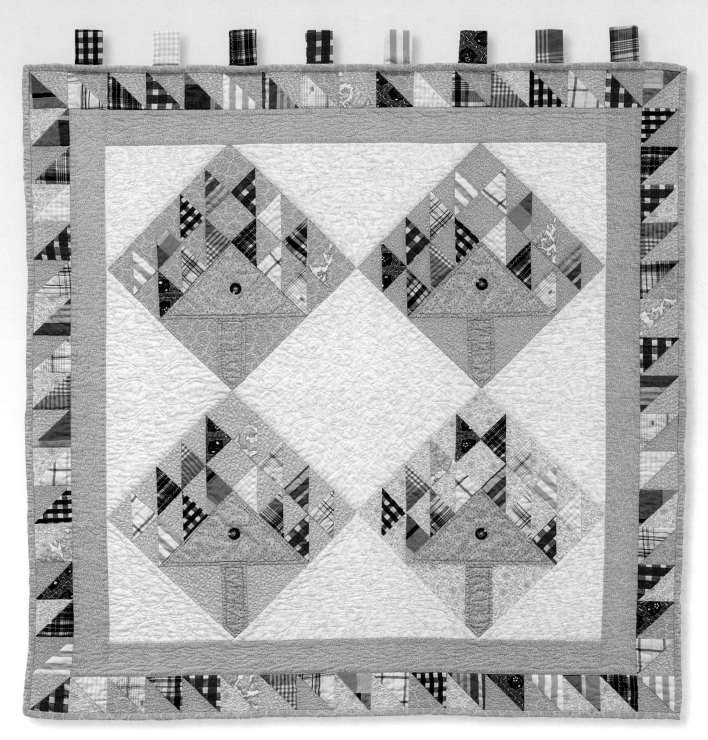

Pieced and quilted by Amy Sandrin.

Finished quilt: 36" x 36" ❖ **Finished block:** 10" x 10"

This quilt was made for a raffle at the semiannual Bellm family reunion. My mom loved this quilt. She wanted this quilt. She knew every detail and every stitch that went into it as if she had made it herself. Because it was created using Grandma Bellm's dresses, all eight of her children's names were placed in a basket. One of Grandma's great-grandchildren had the honor of pulling the winning name out of the basket. When my mom's name was called, she burst into tears. I think Grandma had a hand in ensuring that Mom went home with the prize she coveted so much.

—Amy

MATERIALS

Yardage is based on 42"-wide fabric unless otherwise noted.

⅝ yard *each* of 4 assorted light to medium beige fabrics for Tree of Life blocks and outer border half-square-triangle squares

⅞ yard of white fabric for unpieced blocks and setting triangles

¾ yard of medium beige fabric for inner border and binding

⅝ yard *total* of assorted dress fabrics for Tree of Life blocks, outer border half-square-triangle units, and hanging tabs

⅜ yard of green fabric for Tree of Life blocks

1⅜ yards of fabric for backing

43" x 43" piece of batting

Muslin or light-colored fabric, cut to desired size, for a quilt label

4 buttons

CUTTING

All measurements include ¼" seam allowances.

From *each* of the 4 assorted light to medium beige fabrics, cut:

❖ 2 strips (8 total), 2⅞" x 42"; crosscut into 15 squares (60 total), 2⅞" x 2⅞". Cut an additional 2 squares from any of the leftover strips for a total of 62 squares.

❖ 1 square (4 total), 6¼" x 6¼"; cut each square twice diagonally to yield 16 quarter-square triangles. You will use 2 triangles from each fabric. Discard the remaining triangles or set them aside for another project.

❖ 2 squares (8 total), 2½" x 2½"

From the assorted dress fabrics, cut a *total* of:

❖ 62 squares, 2⅞" x 2⅞"

❖ 8 pairs of rectangles, 2½" x 5½" (cut each pair from the same fabric)

From the green fabric, cut:

❖ 1 strip, 6⅞" x 42"; crosscut into 2 squares, 6⅞" x 6⅞". Cut each square once diagonally to yield 4 half-square triangles. From the remainder of the strip, cut 4 rectangles, 1⅞" x 5".

From the white fabric, cut:

- 1 square, 15½" x 42"; cut the square twice diagonally to yield 4 side setting triangles
- 1 square, 10½" x 10½"
- 2 squares, 8" x 8"; cut the squares once diagonally to yield 4 corner setting triangles

From the medium beige fabric for inner border and binding, cut:

- 2 strips, 2½" x 28½"
- 2 strips, 2½" x 32½"
- 4 strips, 2¼" x 42"

MAKING THE BLOCKS

1. Use a sharp pencil or marking tool to draw a line from corner to corner on the wrong side of each assorted beige 2⅞" square. Place each marked square right sides together with an assorted dress fabric 2⅞" square. Sew ¼" from both sides of the marked lines. Cut the squares apart on the marked lines. Each layered square will yield two half-square-triangle units. Press the seams toward the darker fabric. Make 124.

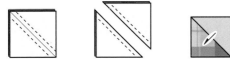

Make 124.

2. Sew matching assorted beige 6¼" quarter-square triangles to the long sides of each green rectangle. The ends of the rectangle will extend beyond the sides of the triangles. Press the seams toward the triangles. Sew this unit to a green triangle as shown. Press the seam toward the green triangle. Trim the excess rectangle even with the sides of the square. Make four.

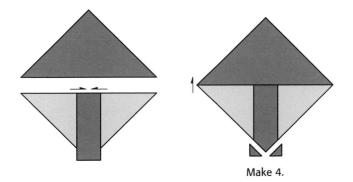

Make 4.

3. Using pieces with the same beige fabric, arrange a unit from step 2, 14 half-square-triangle units, and two 2½" squares into rows as shown. Sew the pieces in each row together. Press the seams in the directions indicated. Sew the rows together to make each section, and then sew the sections to the unit from step 2. Make four blocks. Set the remaining half-square-triangle units aside for the outer border.

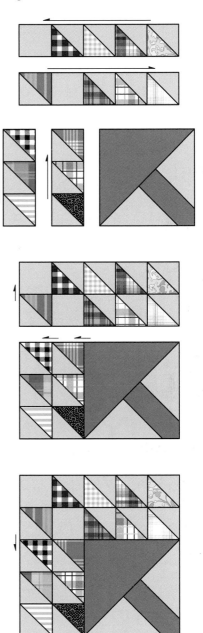

Make 4.

ASSEMBLING THE QUILT

1. Lay out the blocks, the white 10½" square, and the setting triangles into diagonal rows as shown.

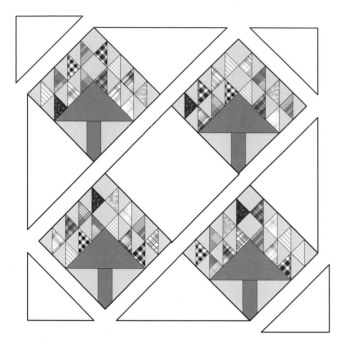

2. Sew the blocks and triangles in each row together. Press all the seams in one row in the same direction, alternating the pressing direction from row to row.

3. Sew a corner setting triangle to each corner of the quilt top.

4. Because the setting triangles were cut a little larger than needed, you will need to trim off the excess ¼" from the block points.

ADDING THE BORDERS

1. Sew the medium beige 2½" x 28½" strips to the top and bottom edges of the quilt top. Press the seams toward the borders.

2. Sew the medium beige 2½" x 32½" strips to the sides of the quilt top. Press the seams toward the borders.

3. Arrange the remaining half-square-triangle units into rows as shown. Sew the squares in each row together. Make one of each row. Press the seams in one direction.

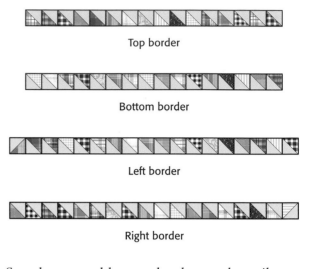

Top border

Bottom border

Left border

Right border

4. Sew the top and bottom borders to the quilt top. Press the seams toward the inner border. Sew the side borders to the quilt top. Press the seams toward the inner border.

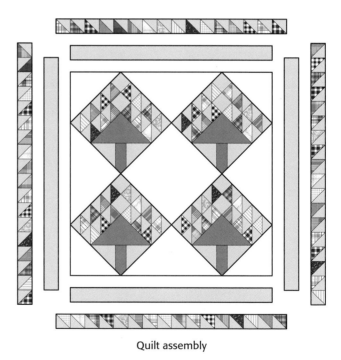

Quilt assembly

FINISHING THE QUILT

Refer to "Finishing Your Quilt" on pages 17–19 for detailed information on finishing techniques.

1. Cut the quilt backing so that it is approximately 6" longer and 6" wider than the quilt top.

2. Layer the quilt top, batting, and backing; baste the layers together.

3. Hand or machine quilt as desired. This quilt was machine quilted using a feather pattern in the un-pieced white block and setting triangles. Around the trees, a tiny stipple, free-motion pattern was used. The leaves in the trees were left unquilted to make them pop out in relief from the tree.

4. Place each pair of dress fabric 2½" x 5½" rectangles right sides together. Sew ¼" from each long edge. Turn the rectangles to the right sides. Press. Make eight.

Make 8.

5. Press the rectangles in half, aligning the raw edges.

6. With the top and tab raw edges aligned, pin the tabs to the back of the quilt top, spacing them evenly across the top edge.

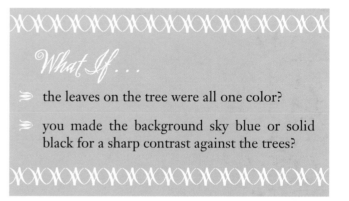

Back of quilt

7. Bind the quilt with the medium beige 2¼"-wide strips, securing the tabs at the same time.

8. Sew a button to the center of each tree.

9. Label the quilt and enjoy a private reunion every time you look at your wall hanging.

What If...

➤ the leaves on the tree were all one color?

➤ you made the background sky blue or solid black for a sharp contrast against the trees?

Three-Dog Night

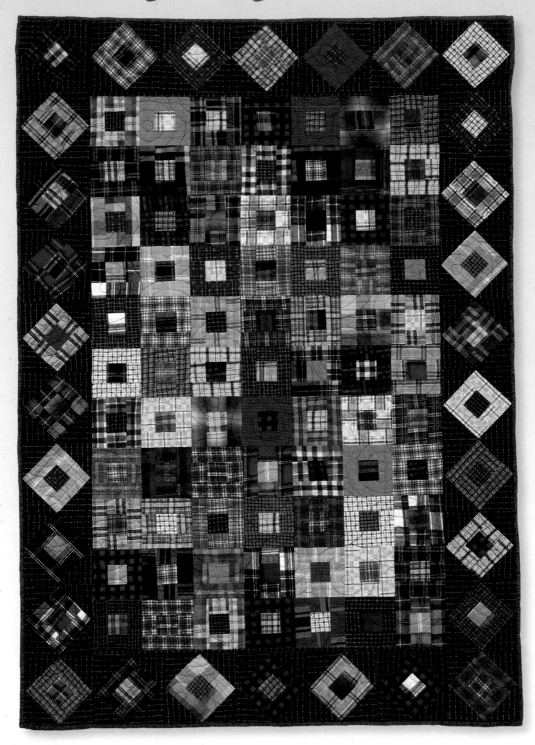

Pieced and quilted by Ann Frischkorn.

Finished quilt: 50" x 71" ❖ **Finished center block: 5" x 5"** ❖ **Finished border block: 7" x 7"**

The expression "three-dog night" describes a night so cold it would take three dogs in your bed to keep you warm. This flannel quilt is so cozy you can forgo the three dogs. In the winter, this is the most sought-after quilt in my house. I used old flannel shirts donated by family and friends. You can use less or more of a variety of flannels, depending on how scrappy you want the quilt to look.

—Ann

MATERIALS

Yardage is based on 38"-wide flannel fabric unless otherwise noted.

5 yards *total* of assorted flannels for quilt center blocks

2 yards of navy blue flannel for border blocks

¾ yard of dark green flannel for binding

3¼ yards of flannel for backing

55" x 76" piece of batting

Muslin or light-colored fabric, cut to desired size, for a quilt label

CUTTING

All measurements include ½" seam allowances.

From the assorted flannels, cut:

- 107 squares, 3" x 3"
- 107 sets consisting of 2 rectangles, 2½" x 3", and 2 rectangles, 2½" x 6". Each set should be cut from the same flannel.

From the navy blue flannel, cut:

- 2 strips, 1½" x 42"
- 9 strips, 6" x 42"; crosscut the strips into 60 squares, 6" x 6". Cut each square once diagonally to yield 120 triangles.

From the dark green flannel, cut:

- 7 strips, 3" x 42"

> **Reminder:** *Because you're working with flannel, use a ½" seam allowance to sew the pieces together.*

MAKING THE BLOCKS

1. Select the pieces for each quilt-center block and separate them into stacks. Each block consists of one 3" square and two *each* of matching 2½" x 3" and 2½" x 6" rectangles. The rectangles should contrast sharply with the square.

2. For each block, sew the 2½" x 3" rectangles to the top and bottom of the 3" square. Press the seams open. Sew the 2½" x 6" rectangles to the sides. Press the seams open. Make 107 Square-in-a-Square blocks.

Square-in-a-Square block.
Make 107.

3. To make the border blocks, sew a navy triangle to opposite sides of 30 of the Square-in-a-Square blocks. Press the seams open. Sew a navy triangle to the remaining two sides. Press the seams open. Trim the blocks to 8" square.

Border block.
Make 30.

ASSEMBLING THE QUILT

1. Lay out the remaining 77 Square-in-a-Square blocks into 11 horizontal rows of 7 blocks each. If possible, arrange the blocks on a design wall so you can stand back and make sure you like the color arrangement.

2. Sew the blocks in each row together. Press the seams open. Sew the rows together. Press the seams open.

ADDING THE BORDER

1. Measure the width of the quilt top through the center. Trim two navy 1½"-wide strips to this measurement and sew them to the top and bottom of the quilt top. Press the seams open.

2. To make the top and bottom borders, sew five border blocks together. Press the seams open. Make two. Sew the borders to the top and bottom edges of the quilt top. Press the seams open.

3. To make the side borders, sew 10 border blocks together. Press the seams open. Make two. Sew the borders to the sides of the quilt top. Press the seams open.

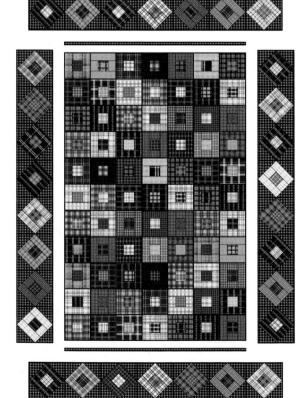

Quilt assembly

FINISHING THE QUILT

Refer to "Finishing Your Quilt" on pages 17–19 for detailed information on finishing techniques.

1. Cut the quilt backing so that it is approximately 6" longer and 6" wider than the quilt top.

2. Layer the quilt top, batting, and backing; baste the layers together.

3. Hand or machine quilt as desired. This quilt was machine quilted with concentric circles.

4. Bind the quilt with the dark green strips.

5. Label the quilt and stay warm and cozy on those "three-dog nights."

What If...

➢ you used only two colors?

➢ you combined flannel with old blue jeans?

➢ you put the seams on the front of the quilt and let them fray?

➢ you combined homespuns and flannels?

You Say Goodbye, I Say Hello

Pieced and quilted by Amy Sandrin.

Finished quilt: 60" x 64"   ❖   **Finished block:** 16" x 16"

35

In the middle of writing this book, I moved from Colorado to Washington State. I traded in the Rocky Mountains for the mountains of the Pacific Northwest. While the two states have their differences, they share a lot of qualities, such as the abundant forests and wildlife. I tried to capture the essence of both in this quilt, using recycled flannel shirts.

—Amy

MATERIALS

Yardage is based on 38"-wide fabric unless otherwise noted.

1⅝ yards of light blue flannel for Tree blocks

1⅝ yards *total* of assorted green plaid flannels for Tree blocks

1¼ yards *total* of assorted plaid flannels for Bear's Paw blocks

1¼ yards of beige flannel for Bear's Paw blocks

¼ *each* of 5 different solid flannels for Bear's Paw block borders

¼ yard of dark green flannel for Bear's Paw blocks

1⅛ yards of dark blue flannel for outer border

⅝ yard of medium brown flannel for middle border

¾ yard of green plaid homespun fabric for binding

3⅝ yards of flannel for backing

66" x 70" piece of batting

Template plastic

Muslin or light-colored fabric, cut to desired size, for a quilt label

CUTTING

All measurements include ½" seam allowances. Before you begin cutting, trace patterns A–H on pages 40–43 onto template plastic and cut them out. Use the templates to cut out the pieces as indicated.

From the light blue flannel, cut:

❖ 6 strips, 5" x 38". From the strips, cut:
  - 4 template A pieces
  - 4 template A reversed pieces
  - 4 template C pieces
  - 4 template C reversed pieces
  - 4 template E pieces
  - 4 template E reversed pieces

❖ 2 strips, 4½" x 38". From the strips, cut:
  - 4 template G pieces
  - 4 template G reversed pieces

❖ 3 strips, 3¾" x 38"; crosscut the strips into 24 squares, 3¾" x 3¾"

From the assorted green plaid flannels, cut a *total* of:

- 4 template B pieces
- 4 template B reversed pieces
- 4 template D pieces
- 4 template D reversed pieces
- 4 template F pieces
- 4 template F reversed pieces
- 4 template H pieces
- 4 template H reversed pieces
- 24 squares, 3¾" x 3¾"

From the beige flannel, cut:

- 80 squares, 3" x 3"
- 40 squares, 3¾" x 3¾"

From the assorted plaid flannels, cut a *total* of:

- 20 sets, consisting of 2 squares, 3¾" x 3¾", and 4 squares, 3" x 3". Each set should be cut from the same plaid fabric.

From the dark green flannel, cut:

- 5 squares, 3" x 3"

From *each* of the 5 different solid flannels, cut:

- 2 strips, 2" x 15"
- 2 strips, 2" x 17"

From the medium brown flannel, cut:

- 6 strips, 3" x 38"

From the dark blue flannel, cut:

- 7 strips, 5" x 38"

From the green plaid homespun fabric, cut:

- 7 strips, 2¾" x 38"

> **Reminder:** *Because you're working with flannel, use a ½" seam allowance to sew the pieces together.*

MAKING THE TREE BLOCKS

1. Sew the light blue template pieces to the assorted green plaid template pieces as shown to make the Tree-block units. Make four of each unit.

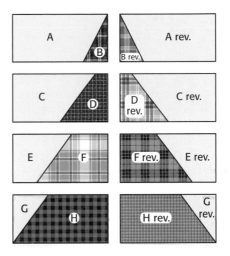

2. Arrange one of each unit into four rows as shown. Sew the units in each row together. Press the seams in alternate directions from row to row. Sew the rows together. Make four Tree blocks.

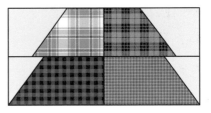
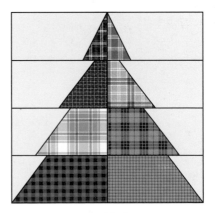

Tree block.
Make 4.

MAKING THE BEAR'S PAW BLOCKS

1. Use a sharp pencil or marking tool to draw a line from corner to corner on the wrong side of each beige 3¾" square. Place each marked square right sides together with an assorted plaid 3¾" square (do not use the green plaid squares at this time). Sew ½" from both sides of the marked lines. Cut the squares apart on the marked lines. Each layered square will yield two half-square-triangle units. Press the seams toward the plaid fabric. Make 20 sets of four matching half-square-triangle units (80 total).

Make 20 sets
of 4 each.

2. Arrange 16 beige 3" squares, 1 dark green 3" square, 16 matching half-square-triangle units, and 16 plaid 3" squares that match the half-square-triangle units into seven horizontal rows as shown. Sew the squares in each row together. Press the seams in each row in one direction. Press the seams in opposite directions from row to row. Sew the rows together. Press the seams in one direction. Make five.

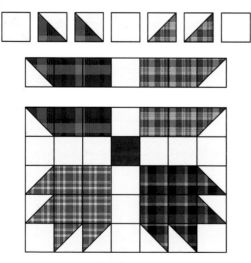

Make 5.

3. Sew matching solid flannel 2" x 15" strips to the top and bottom of each step 2 unit. Press the seams toward the strips. Sew the matching solid flannel 2" x 17" strips to the sides of each unit. Press the seams toward the strips to complete the five Bear's Paw blocks.

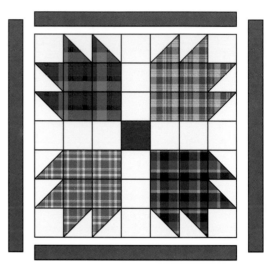

Bear's Paw block.
Make 5.

ASSEMBLING THE QUILT

1. Refer to the assembly diagram to lay out the blocks in three horizontal rows of three blocks each, alternating the Bear's Paw blocks with the Tree blocks as shown on page 39.

2. Sew the blocks in each row together. Press the seams in one row in the same direction, alternating the pressing direction from row to row. Sew the rows together. Press the seams in one direction.

ADDING THE BORDERS

1. Use a sharp pencil or marking tool to draw a line from corner to corner on the wrong side of each light blue 3¾" square. Place each marked square right sides together with an assorted green plaid 3¾" square. Sew ½" from both sides of the marked lines. Cut the squares apart on the marked lines. Each layered square will yield two half-square-triangle units. Press the seams toward the plaid fabric. Make 48.

2. Sew 24 half-square-triangle units together into one horizontal row as shown. Press the seams in one direction. Make two rows.

Make 2.

3. Sew the rows to the top and bottom edges of the quilt top so that the points are facing up. Press the seams toward the blocks.

4. Piece the brown 3" x 38" strips together end to end. From the pieced strip, cut two strips, 3" x 49", for the top and bottom borders, and two strips, 3" x 53", for the side borders.

> *Note: Because flannel stretches so much, it's better to use the measurement of what the blocks should be, following the cutting instructions, instead of using the actual center measurements.*

5. Sew the top and bottom borders to the top and bottom edges of the quilt top. Press the seams toward the borders. Sew the side borders to the sides of the quilt top. Press the seams toward the borders.

6. Piece the dark blue 5" x 38" strips together end to end. From the pieced strip, cut two strips, 5" x 53", for the top and bottom borders, and two strips, 5" x 65", for the side borders.

7. Sew the top and bottom borders to the quilt top. Press the seams toward the borders. Sew the side borders to the quilt top. Press the seams toward the borders.

Quilt assembly

FINISHING THE QUILT

Refer to "Finishing Your Quilt" on pages 17–19 for detailed information on finishing techniques.

1. Piece the quilt backing so that it is approximately 6" longer and 6" wider than the quilt top.

2. Layer the quilt top, batting, and backing; baste the layers together.

3. Hand or machine quilt as desired. This quilt was quilted with an overall free-motion design that resembles a cross between flower petals and clamshells.

4. Bind the quilt with the homespun strips.

5. Label the quilt and enjoy nature no matter where you live.

What If...

➢ you used red and green fabrics for the Bear's Paw blocks and blue snowflake fabric for the Tree block backgrounds and sewed beads on the trees for Christmas ornaments?

➢ you used silk fabric for the trees so that the "needles" shimmered?

39

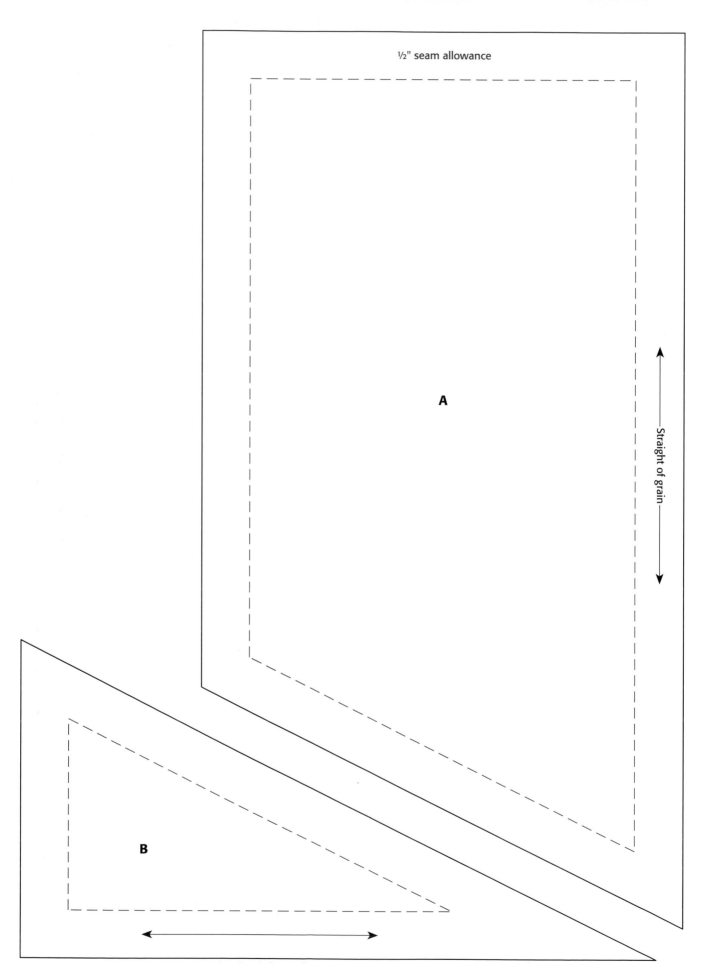

½" seam allowance

A

Straight of grain

B

40

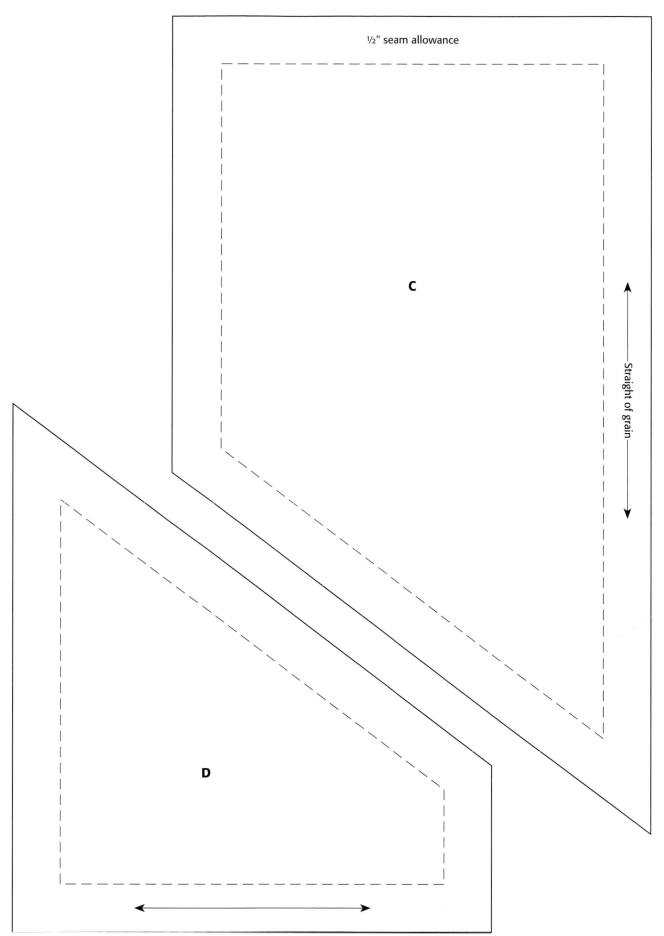

½" seam allowance

C

Straight of grain

D

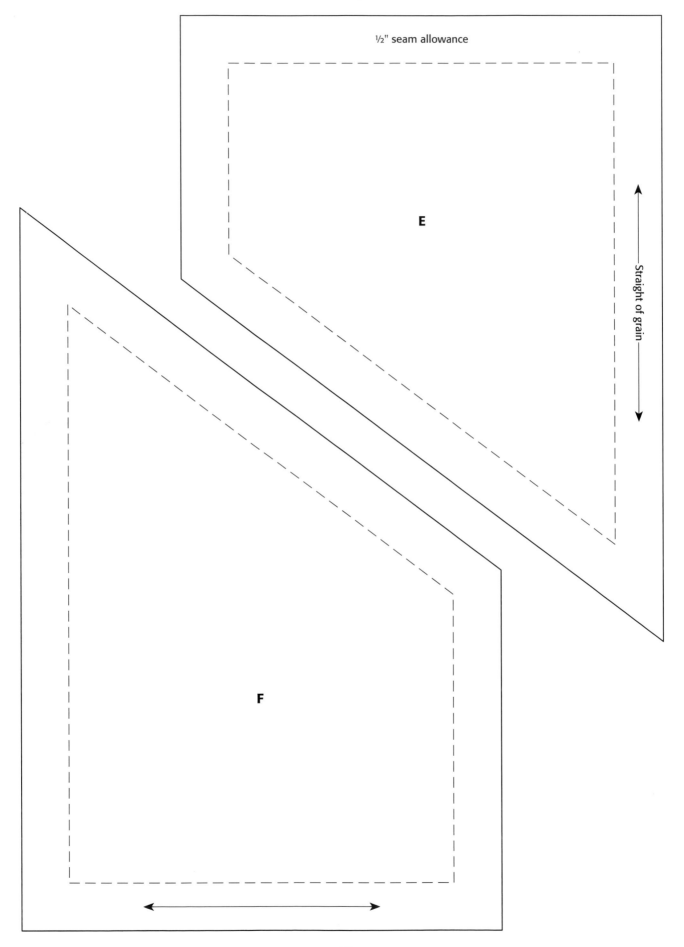

½" seam allowance

E

Straight of grain

F

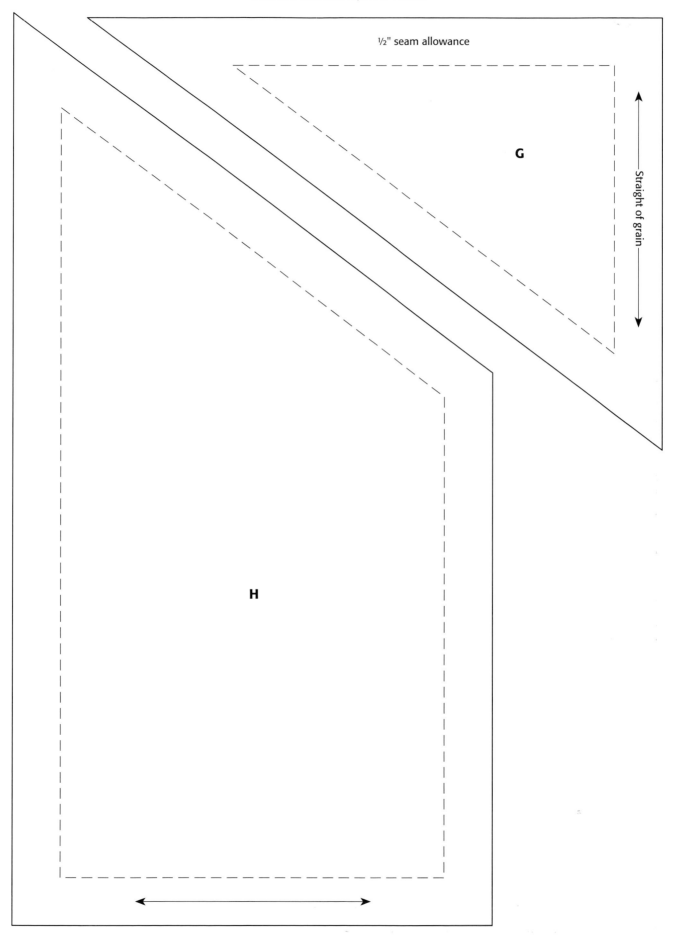

½" seam allowance

Straight of grain

G

H

43

Bursting at the Seams

Pieced and quilted by Ann Frischkorn.

Finished quilt: 25" x 25" ❖ **Finished block: 7" x 7"**

I made the sunburst points in this wall hanging with my husband's discarded neckties, which, according to him, were no longer in style. The background fabric looks like dress shirts, but it's actually 100% cotton purchased from a quilt shop. It's fun to combine vintage fabric with new fabric and discover how well they can blend.

—*Ann*

MATERIALS

Yardage is based on 42"-wide fabric unless otherwise noted.

⅜ yard *each* of 9 assorted light fabrics for blocks (select fabrics that look like men's dress shirts)

9 men's neckties OR ⅛ yard *each* of 9 assorted dark fabrics for block sunbursts and borders

⅜ yard of dark blue fabric for binding

1 yard of fabric for backing

31" x 31" piece of batting

Papers for foundation piecing

2¼ yards of 22"-wide lightweight fusible interfacing

1⅛ yards of 22"-wide lightweight nonfusible interfacing

1 package of tear-away stabilizer

3½" square of template plastic

Muslin or light-colored fabric, cut to desired size, for a quilt label

CUTTING

All measurements include ¼" seam allowances. Before cutting the ties, refer to "Men's Tie Fabrics" on page 12 for information on how to take apart the ties and interface them. Label the ties 1–9.

From *each* of the 9 light fabrics, cut:

❖ 1 strip, 7½" x 42"; crosscut the strip into 1 square, 7½" x 7½". From the remainder of the strip, cut 1 strip, 2½" x 32".

From *each* of the 9 interfaced ties or 9 assorted dark fabrics, cut:

❖ 1 square, 3½" x 3½"
❖ 2 strips, 2½" x length of tie strips

From the remainder of tie 1, cut:

❖ 2 rectangles, 2½" x 5½"

From the remainder of *each* of ties 2 and 6, cut:

❖ 1 rectangle, 2½" x 7½"

From the remainder of tie 3, cut:

❖ 1 rectangle, 2½" x 5½"
❖ 1 rectangle, 2½" x 3½"

From the remainder of tie 4, cut:

❖ 1 rectangle, 2½" x 7½"
❖ 1 rectangle, 2½" x 6½"
❖ 1 rectangle, 2½" x 4½"

From the remainder of tie 5, cut:

❖ 1 rectangle, 2½" x 7½"
❖ 1 rectangle, 2½" x 6½"

From the remainder of tie 7, cut:

❖ 1 rectangle, 2½" x 7½"
❖ 1 rectangle, 2½" x 6½"

From the remainder of tie 8, cut:

- ❖ 1 rectangle, 2½" x 7½"
- ❖ 1 rectangle, 2½" x 4½"

From the remainder of tie 9, cut:

- ❖ 1 rectangle, 2½" x 6½"

From the nonfusible interfacing, cut:

- ❖ 2 strips, 3½" x 22"; crosscut into 9 squares, 3½" x 3½"
- ❖ 3 strips, 7" x 22"; crosscut into 9 squares, 7" x 7"

From the dark blue fabric, cut:

- ❖ 3 strips, 2¼" x 42"

MAKING THE BLOCKS

1. To make the sunburst-point units, cut each of the light 2½" x 32" strips into 24 triangles with a base of 2" as shown. These will be used for the odd-numbered sections of the paper-piecing units.

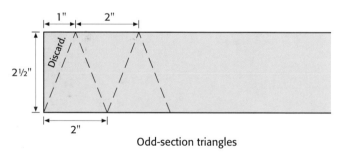

Odd-section triangles

2. Cut each the 2½"-wide tie strips into 20 triangles with a base of 1½" as shown. These will be used for the even-numbered sections of the paper-piecing units.

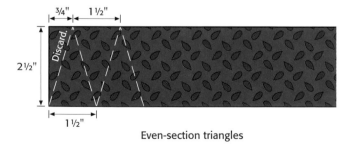

Even-section triangles

3. Refer to "Paper-Piecing Instructions" on pages 15 and 16 to make 36 sunburst-point foundation patterns, using the pattern on page 48.

4. Paper piece the units, using the appropriate triangles cut in steps 1 and 2 for the odd- and even-numbered sections. You will need four units made from the same fabrics for each block. Do not remove the paper foundations yet.

5. Sew four units together as shown to form a circle. Make nine.

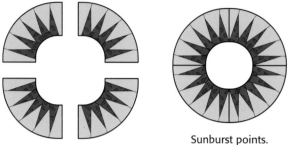

Sunburst points.
Make 9.

6. Trace the circle pattern on page 48 onto template plastic and cut it out.

7. Lay the circle template on the wrong side of a 3½" tie square and trace around it. If the tie has been interfaced, the circle will be drawn on the interfacing.

8. Lay the marked tie square, wrong side up, on top of a 3½" nonfusible interfacing square; pin together on all four sides. Stitch on the traced circle using 15 stitches per inch. Overlap the stitches at the beginning and end to secure them.

9. Trim the circle ⅛" from the stitching line. Cut a small slit in the center of the interfacing, being careful not to cut the tie fabric underneath. Turn the circle right side out and gently push out the edges with a blunt instrument, such as a crochet hook.

10. Using a dry iron on a low setting, press the circle from the fabric side only, making sure the interfacing does not show from the front. Trim the interfacing from the back, leaving about ¼" seam allowance around the edges.

11. Because the centers of the sunburst-point units are an empty hole, they need to be stabilized so the coordinating 3" circles can be attached. Place a 6" square of tear-away stabilizer on the wrong side of

each sunburst-point unit. Center and pin the coordinating 3" tie circle on the right side of each unit, making sure to catch the stabilizer with the pins.

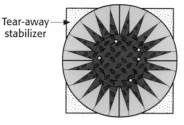

Pin 3" circle over points.

12. Stitch the 3" circle into place using a blind hem stitch. I found that smoke nylon thread in the top and a light gray all-purpose thread in the bobbin worked great for all the tie colors.

13. Remove the tear-away stabilizer from the back, but do not remove the paper-piecing paper yet.

14. Place a 7" square of nonfusible interfacing on the right side of your sunburst unit and pin it in place. Using 15 stitches per inch, stitch along the ¼" seam line around the outside of the circle.

15. Remove the paper-piecing paper. Use tweezers to help remove the paper from the small areas.

16. Cut a slit in the center of the interfacing, being careful not to cut the fabric underneath it. Turn the circle to the right side; press, making sure the interfacing does not show from the front. Trim the interfacing from the back, leaving about ¼" seam allowance around the edges.

17. Center and pin the sunburst unit to a 7½" square of light fabric. Stitch the circle into place using a blind hem stitch and clear nylon thread. If desired, cut away the light fabric behind the sunburst unit, being very careful not to cut the sunburst.

ASSEMBLING THE QUILT

1. Refer to the assembly diagram to lay out the blocks in three horizontal rows of three blocks each. Rearrange the blocks until the color placement is pleasing.

2. Sew the blocks in each row together. Press the seams of each row in the same direction, alternating the pressing direction from row to row. Sew the rows together. Press the seams in one direction.

ADDING THE BORDER

1. Assemble the tie rectangles into border strips as shown.

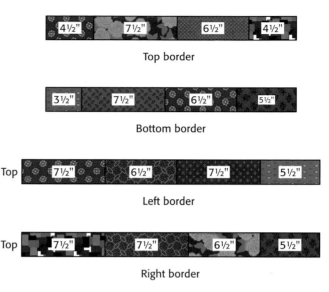

2. Sew the top and bottom borders to the quilt top. Press the seams toward the borders. Sew the side borders to the quilt top. Press the seams toward the borders.

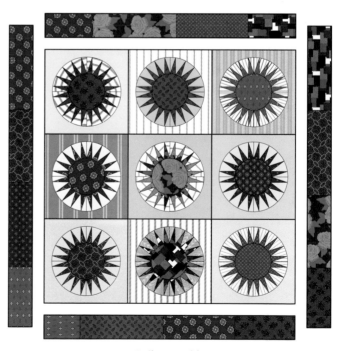

Quilt assembly

47

FINISHING THE QUILT

Refer to "Finishing Your Quilt" on pages 17–19 for detailed information on finishing techniques.

1. Cut the quilt backing so that it is approximately 6" longer and 6" wider than the quilt top.

2. Layer the quilt top, batting, and backing; baste the layers together.

3. Hand or machine quilt as desired. This quilt was machine quilted with overall stippling in the background. The sunburst tie portions were left unquilted.

4. Bind the quilt with the dark blue strips.

5. Label the quilt and enjoy the fact that you brought out-of-date ties back into vogue.

What If . . .

⇒ you used different fabrics for each point, giving the quilt a very scrappy look?

⇒ you used two colors, one light for the background and one dark for the sunbursts, or one dark for the background and one light for the sunbursts?

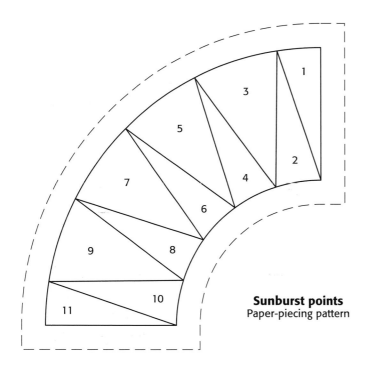

Sunburst points
Paper-piecing pattern

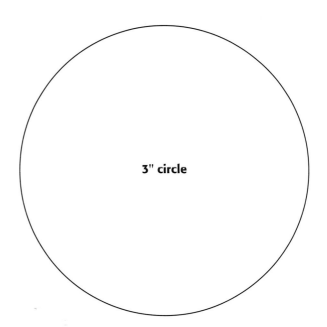

3" circle

Tied Up in Court

Pieced and quilted by Amy Sandrin.

Finished quilt: 53" x 65" ❖ **Finished block:** 12" x 12"

One of the first places we went to find donation ties for this book was my brother-in-law's law firm in downtown Chicago. When the office decided to allow business casual attire and only require ties when necessary (that is, when the lawyers were in court), the lawyers were only too happy to part with their "neck nooses" for the worthy cause of a quilt project. Because this block is a variation of the Courthouse Steps pattern, and the lawyers only wear ties in court, what else could I call this quilt but "Tied Up in Court"?

—Amy

MATERIALS

Yardage is based on 42"-wide fabric unless otherwise noted.

2¼ yards *total* of assorted dark tie fabrics for blocks (roughly 20 ties, more if you want a wider variety)

2¼ yards *total* of assorted light-colored fabrics for blocks (use approximately 20 different fabrics for variety)

1¼ yards of red fabric for blocks and inner border

⅝ yard of light green fabric for outer border

⅝ yard of dark green fabric for binding

3½ yards of fabric for backing

59" x 71" piece of batting

3⅛ yards of 22"-wide lightweight fusible interfacing

Muslin or light-colored fabric, cut to desired size, for a quilt label

CUTTING

All measurements include ¼" seam allowances. Before cutting the ties, refer to "Men's Tie Fabrics" on page 12 for information on how to take the ties apart and interface them.

From the red fabric, cut:

- 16 strips, 1½" x 42"; crosscut the strips into 400 squares, 1½" x 1½"
- 2 strips, 2½" x 42"; crosscut the strips into 20 squares, 2½" x 2½"
- 6 strips, ¾" x 42"

From the assorted light-colored fabrics, cut a *total* of:

- 40 rectangles, 1½" x 2½"
- 40 rectangles, 1½" x 4½"
- 40 rectangles, 1½" x 6½"
- 40 rectangles, 1½" x 8½"
- 40 rectangles, 1½" x 10½"

From the interfaced assorted dark tie fabrics, cut a *total* of:

- 40 rectangles, 1½" x 2½"
- 40 rectangles, 1½" x 4½"
- 40 rectangles, 1½" x 6½"
- 40 rectangles, 1½" x 8½"
- 40 rectangles, 1½" x 10½"

From *each* of 4 of the interfaced assorted dark tie fabrics, cut:

- 1 square, 3" x 3"

From the light green fabric, cut:

- 6 strips, 3" x 42"

From the dark green fabric, cut:

- 7 strips, 2¼" x 42"

MAKING THE BLOCKS

1. Sew a red 1½" square to each end of all of the light-colored rectangles. Press the seams toward the rectangles.

2. Sew a 1½" x 2½" tie rectangle to the sides of a red 2½" square. Press the seams away from the square. This is the beginning of the block. We will continue to build around this.

3. Sew a light-colored 1½" x 2½" rectangle (with the red squares on both ends) to the top and bottom of the block, matching up seams. The more accurately the seams are matched up, the easier this quilt will go together. Press the seams away from the center square.

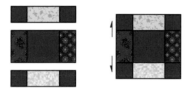

4. Sew a 1½" x 4½" tie rectangle to the sides of the block. Press the seams away from the center square.

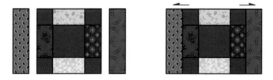

5. Continue going back and forth in this manner, sewing the tie rectangles to the sides and the light rectangles to the top and bottom of the block, each time using the next longest rectangle until five rectangles have been added to each side of the

block. Press the seams away from the center after each addition. Make 20 blocks.

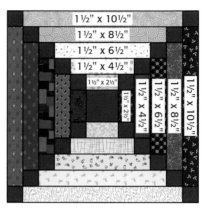

Make 20.

ASSEMBLING THE QUILT

1. Refer to the assembly diagram to lay out the blocks in five horizontal rows of four blocks each as shown on page 52, alternating the direction of the light and dark fabrics.

2. Sew the blocks in each row together. Press all the seams in one row in the same direction, alternating the direction from row to row. Sew the rows together. Press the seams in one direction.

ADDING THE BORDERS

1. Piece the red ¾"-wide strips together end to end to make one long strip.

2. Measure the width of the quilt top through the center. From the pieced strip, cut two strips the length measured. Sew these two strips to the top and bottom edges of the quilt top. Press the seams toward the borders.

3. Measure the length of the quilt top through the center, including the just-added borders. From the remainder of the pieced strip, cut two strips the length measured. Sew these two strips to the sides of the quilt. Press the seam allowances toward the borders.

4. Piece the light green strips together end to end to make one long strip.

51

5. Measure the width of the quilt top through the center. From the pieced strip, cut two strips the length measured for the outer top and bottom borders. Do not sew the strips to the quilt top at this time. Measure the length of the quilt top through the center. From the remainder of the pieced strip, cut two strips the length measured for the side borders.

6. Sew the top and bottom outer-border strips to the quilt top. Press the seams toward the borders.

7. Add a 3" tie square to the ends of each side border strip. Sew the side borders to the quilt top. Press the seams toward the borders.

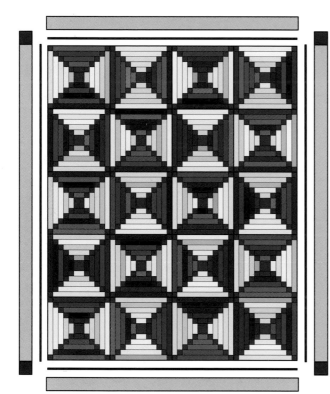

Quilt assembly

FINISHING THE QUILT

Refer to "Finishing Your Quilt" on pages 17–19 for detailed information on finishing techniques.

1. Piece the quilt backing so that it is approximately 6" longer and 6" wider than the quilt top.

2. Layer the quilt top, batting, and backing; baste the layers together.

3. Hand or machine quilt as desired. Because the fabric and pattern in this quilt are so busy, a simple grid pattern was used; anything more intricate would probably not have shown up. Because the quilt contains silk fabric, it is not advisable to mark the pattern on the quilt top.

4. Bind the quilt with the dark green strips.

5. Label the quilt, liberate the ties, and live casual.

What If...

→ you made the quilt with flannel fabrics instead of ties?

→ you arranged the blocks differently? For example, you placed the light sides together.

→ you made the entire quilt with just light and dark ties and eliminated the cotton fabric?

Dancing down Memory Lane

Pieced and quilted by Ann Frischkorn.

Finished quilt: 35" x 42" ◈ **Finished block:** 3½" x 7"

53

This quilt has some very special memories sewn into the seams. The lacy white fabric came from Amy's wedding gown. A purple silk was from a dress I wore to a Chamber of Commerce Snowflake Ball. The brown taffeta was commandeered from a gown Amy wore to an Awards Night Ceremony at the Romance Writers of America annual conference. The hot pink came from a bridesmaid dress worn in a friend's wedding. A green silk was from a dress my mom wore to my brother's wedding. All I have to do is look at this quilt to take a trip down Special-Events Memory Lane.

—Ann

MATERIALS

Yardage is based on 42"-wide fabric unless otherwise noted.

3 yards *total* of assorted silky fabrics for blocks

1⅝ yards of solid black 100%-cotton fabric for "leading," sashing, and borders

½ yard of bright red silky fabric for binding

1⅓ yards of fabric for backing

41" x 48" piece of batting

Papers for foundation piecing

6 yards of 22"-wide lightweight fusible interfacing

Muslin or light-colored fabric, cut to desired size, for a quilt label

CUTTING

All measurements include ¼" seam allowances. Before cutting the silky fabrics, refer to "Silky Fabrics" on page 13 for information on interfacing them.

From the assorted silky fabrics, cut:

- 143 rectangles, 4" x 6"

From the solid black 100%-cotton fabric, cut:

- 17 strips, 1" x 42"; crosscut into:
  - 128 rectangles, 1" x 4¾"
  - 5 rectangles, 1" x 6"
- 7 strips, 1½" x 42"
- 6 strips, 4" x 42"; crosscut into:
  - 1 rectangle, 4" x 29¼"
  - 1 rectangle, 4" x 22½"
  - 1 rectangle, 4" x 19½"
  - 1 rectangle, 4" x 15½"
  - 1 rectangle, 4" x 15"
  - 1 rectangle, 4" x 10½"
  - 2 rectangles, 4" x 9½"
  - 1 rectangle, 4" x 9¼"
  - 9 rectangles, 4" x 6"
  - 1 rectangle, 4" x 4½"

From the bright red silky fabric, cut:

- 5 strips, 2¼" x 40"

MAKING THE BLOCKS

1. Refer to "Paper-Piecing Instructions" on pages 15 and 16 to make five patterns *each* of blocks A–E and one *each* of blocks F–L, using the patterns on pages 57–65.

2. Paper piece four *each* of blocks A–E, using the silky 4" x 6" rectangles for the wide sections. Use the black 1" x 4¾" rectangles for the sections labeled "black," except for block C, section 6, which will require the use of the black 1" x 6" rectangles. Do not remove the paper foundations yet.

3. Paper piece the remaining A–E blocks in the same manner, but eliminate section 10 by treating sections 9 and 10 as one unit and covering them with the same piece of silky fabric. These blocks will be placed at the bottom of rows 1, 2, 4, 5, and 6 when the quilt top rows are assembled. Do not remove the paper foundations yet.

4. Paper piece blocks F–L, using the black 4" x 6" rectangles for the wide sections labeled "black," the black 1" x 4¾" for the narrow sections labeled "black," and the silky 4" x 6" rectangles for the remaining wide sections. Blocks F–H will be used in row 3; blocks I–L will be used in the borders. Do not remove the paper foundations yet.

ASSEMBLING THE QUILT

1. Lay out blocks A–E in five vertical rows of five blocks each, making sure that the five blocks without section 10 are placed at the bottom of each row. It doesn't matter which order the blocks are arranged in. Rearrange them until the color placement is pleasing. Again, remember to keep the designated blocks at the bottom of the rows. When the blocks are arranged in a pleasing order, sew the blocks in each row together. These will be rows 1, 2, 4, 5, and 6.

2. To make row 3, join blocks F, G, and H with the black rectangles indicated as shown at right.

3. Measure one row through the center from top to bottom. Crosscut each of the seven black 1½"-wide strips to this length. These are the sashing strips.

4. Sew the sashing strips and rows together as shown in the assembly diagram on page 56. Press the seams toward the sashing strips.

ADDING THE BORDERS

1. Refer to the illustrations below to join blocks I, J, K, and L with the black rectangles indicated to make the border strips.

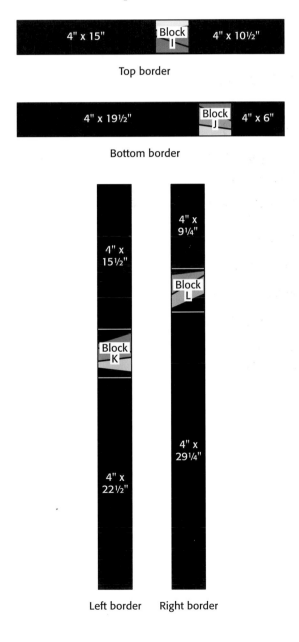

55

2. Sew the top and bottom borders to the top and bottom edges of the quilt top. Press the seams toward the borders.

3. Sew the left and right side borders to the sides of the quilt top. Press the seams toward the borders.

4. Remove the paper foundations.

FINISHING THE QUILT

Refer to "Finishing Your Quilt" on pages 17–19 for detailed information on finishing techniques.

1. Cut the quilt backing so that it is approximately 6" longer and 6" wider than the quilt top.

2. Layer the quilt top, batting, and backing; baste the layers together.

3. Hand or machine quilt as desired. This quilt was machine quilted with black thread, following the black leading. The silk pieces were left unquilted.

Free-form feather motifs were quilted in the large black areas of the sashing and in row 3.

4. Bind the quilt with the red silky fabric strips.

5. Label the quilt and relive all those fancy occasions!

What If . . .

➣ you used batik fabrics instead of silky fabrics?

➣ you used white or light-colored fabric for the background instead of black?

➣ you used a monochromatic color scheme?

Quilt assembly

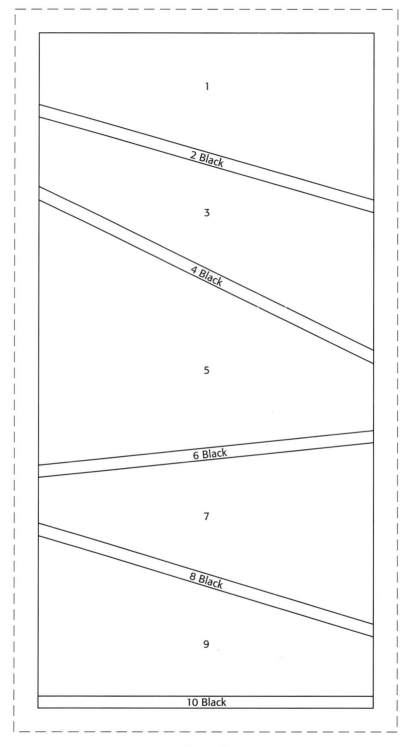

Block A
Paper-piecing pattern

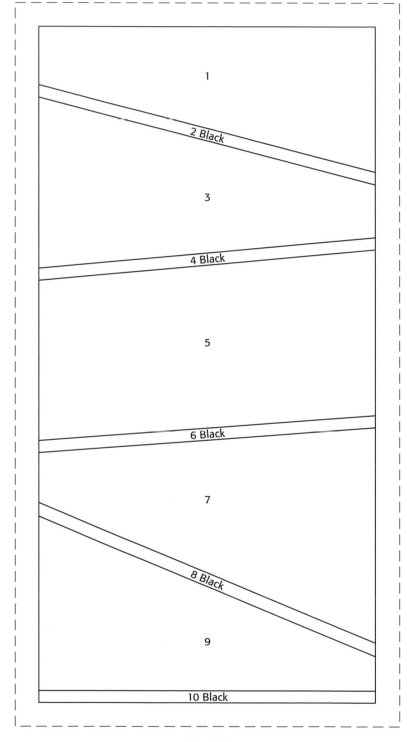

Block B
Paper-piecing pattern

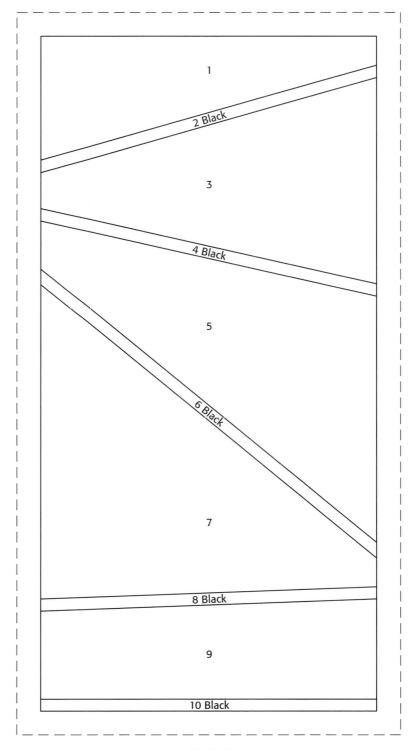

Block C
Paper-piecing pattern

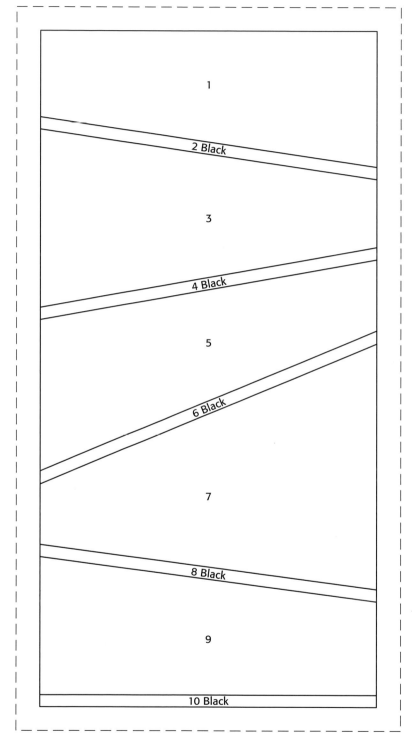

Block D
Paper-piecing pattern

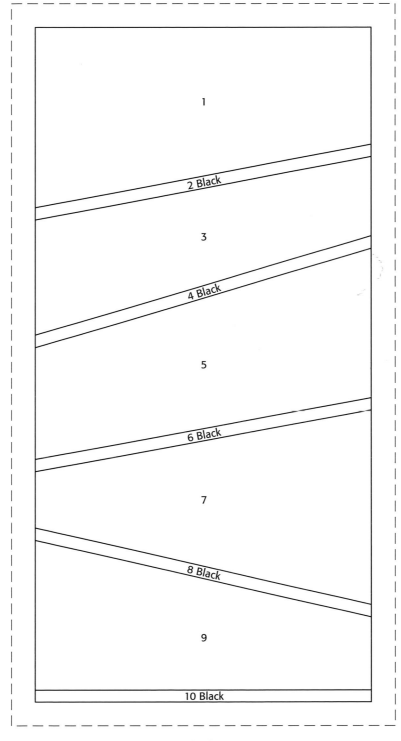

Block E
Paper-piecing pattern

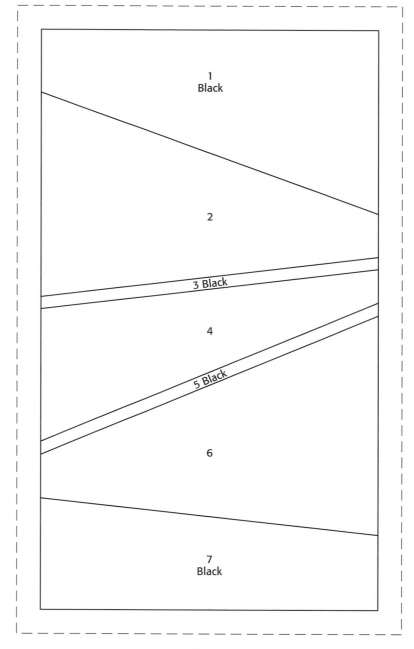

Block F
Paper-piecing pattern

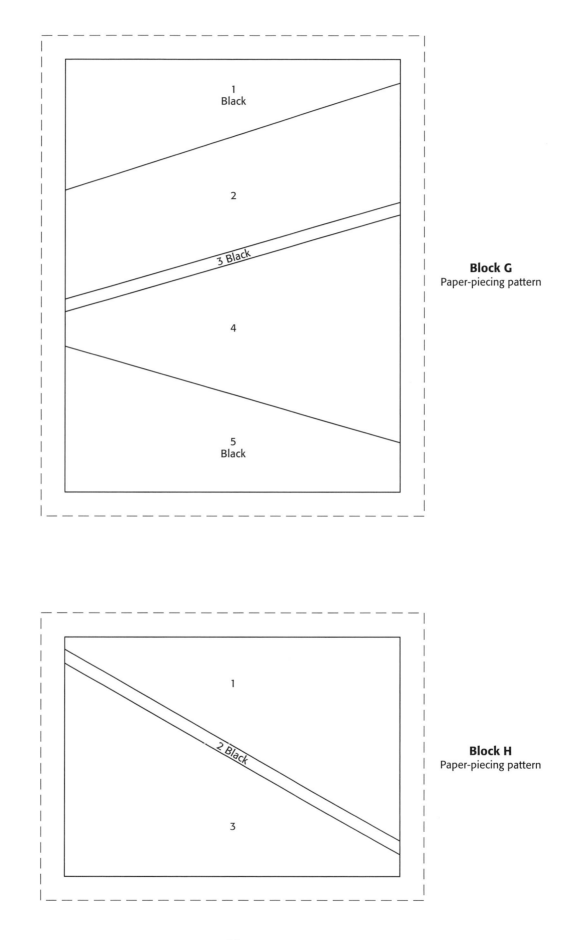

Block G
Paper-piecing pattern

Block H
Paper-piecing pattern

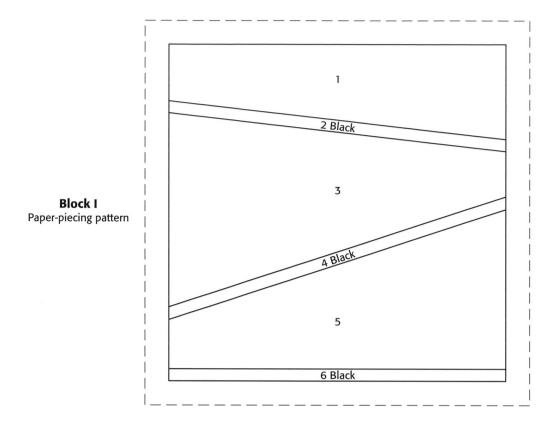

Block I
Paper-piecing pattern

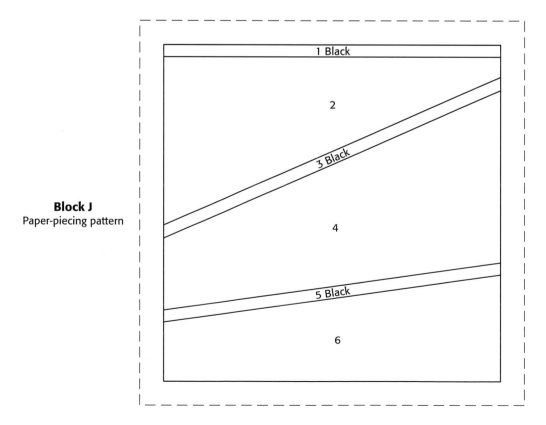

Block J
Paper-piecing pattern

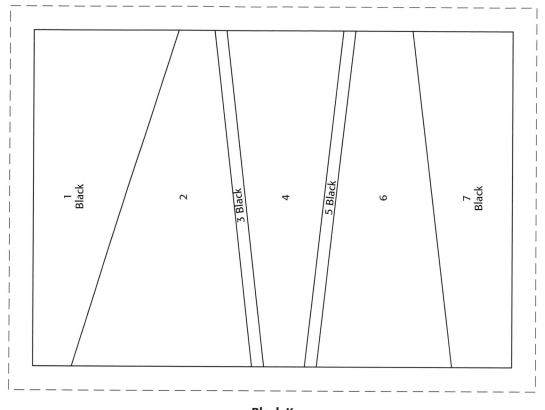

Block K
Paper-piecing pattern

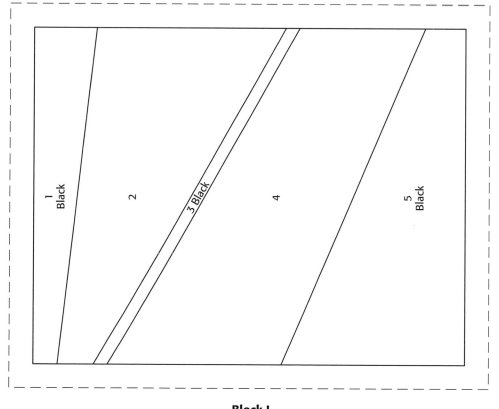

Block L
Paper-piecing pattern

Sure You'll Wear It Again

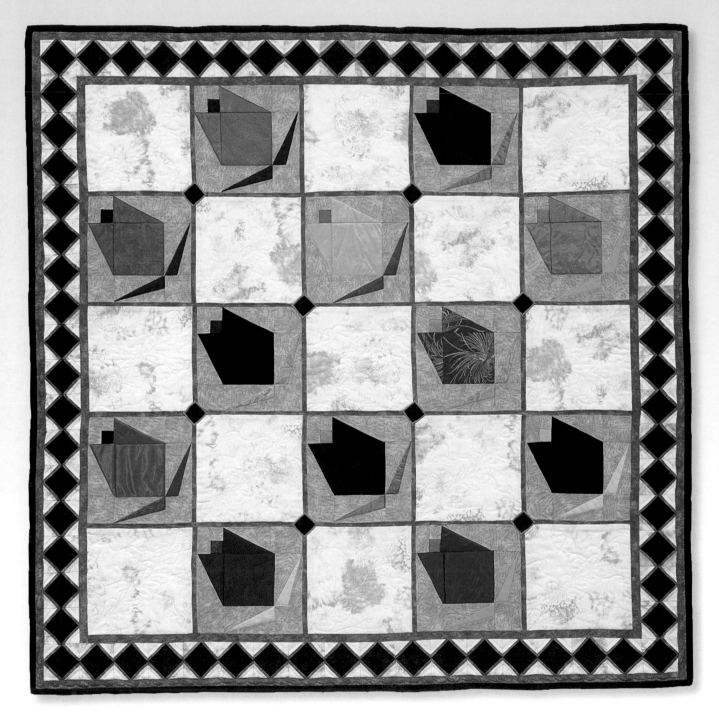

Pieced and quilted by Amy Sandrin.

Finished quilt: 37" x 37" ❖ **Finished block:** 6" x 6"

How many times have you been asked to be a bridesmaid and heard the bride-to-be claim, "I've picked out a dress that you can definitely wear again"? Let's face it, it just doesn't happen. Bridesmaid dresses are meant to be worn only once. I've saved dresses in my closet for years, waiting for an occasion to wear them a second time. When reality dawned, I found a different way to use those dresses again.

—Amy

MATERIALS

Yardage is based on 42"-wide fabric unless otherwise noted.

1½ yards of medium tan fabric for sashing and borders

1¼ yards of white marbled fabric for unpieced blocks and middle pieced border

1⅛ yards of light tan fabric for paper-pieced blocks

¾ yard of dark brown fabric for blocks, borders, and binding

7" x 10" rectangle *each* of 12 assorted silky fabrics for paper-pieced blocks

⅜ yard *total* of assorted green silky fabrics for paper-pieced blocks

1½ yards of fabric for backing

43" x 43" piece of batting

Papers for foundation piecing

1⅛ yards of 22"-wide lightweight fusible interfacing

Muslin or light-colored fabric, cut to desired size, for a quilt label

CUTTING

All measurements include ¼" seam allowances. Before cutting the silky fabrics, refer to "Silky Fabrics" on page 13 for information on interfacing them.

From the light tan fabric, cut:

❖ 2 strips, 1½" x 42"; crosscut into:
  • 12 squares, 1½" x 1½"
  • 12 rectangles, 1½" x 2¼"

❖ 4 strips, 2" x 42"; crosscut into 24 rectangles, 2" x 6½". Cut each rectangle once diagonally from the bottom right to the top left.

❖ 9 strips, 2½" x 42"; crosscut into:
  • 48 rectangles, 2½" x 5"
  • 36 squares, 2½" x 2½"

From *each* of the 12 assorted silky fabric rectangles, cut:

❖ 1 square, 3¾" x 3¾"

❖ 2 rectangles, 2½" x 5"

❖ 1 square, 1½" x 1½"

From the assorted green silky fabrics, cut a *total* of:

❖ 12 pairs of rectangles, 2" x 6½". Each pair should be cut from the same fabric.

From the dark brown fabric, cut:

- 4 strips, 2⅛" x 42"; crosscut into 68 squares, 2⅛" x 2⅛"
- 8 squares, 1" x 1"
- 4 strips, 2¼" x 42"

From the medium tan fabric, cut:

- 7 strips, ¾" x 42"; crosscut into:
  - 4 strips, ¾" x 31½"
  - 20 rectangles, ¾" x 6½"
- 16 strips, 2⅛" x 42"; crosscut into 272 rectangles, ⅞" x 2⅛"
- 8 strips, 1" x 42"

From the white marbled fabric, cut:

- 3 strips, 6½" x 42"; crosscut into 13 squares, 6½" x 6½"
- 8 strips, 2¼" x 42"; crosscut into 136 squares, 2¼" x 2¼". Cut each square once diagonally to yield 272 triangles.

MAKING THE BLOCKS

1. Refer to "Paper-Piecing Instructions" on pages 15 and 16 to make 12 Tile Flower block patterns and 68 Border Square block patterns, using the patterns on pages 69 and 70.

2. Paper piece the three parts of each Tile Flower block, using the fabric pieces indicated on the pattern for each section. Each block will use one color of silky fabric for the areas marked "Silky 1" and a coordinating color of silky fabric for the area marked "Silky 2." Sew the parts together to complete the blocks. Make 12. Do not remove the paper foundations yet.

3. Paper piece the Border Square blocks, using the dark brown 2⅛" squares for section 1, the medium tan ⅞" x 2⅛" rectangles for sections 2–5, and the white triangles for sections 6–9. Do not remove the paper foundations yet.

ASSEMBLING THE QUILT

1. Lay out the Tile Flower blocks, the white 6½" squares, and the medium tan ¾" x 6½" rectangles in five horizontal rows as shown.

2. Sew the pieces in each row together. Press all the seams in one row in the same direction, alternating the direction from row to row.

3. Sew the block rows together, inserting a medium tan ¾" x 31½" sashing strip between each row.

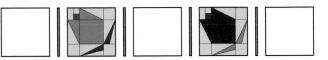

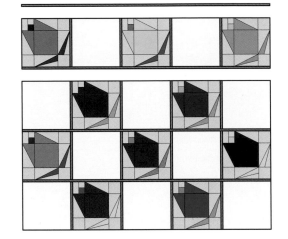

ADDING THE BORDERS

1. Measure the width of the quilt top through the center. Trim two medium tan 1" x 42" strips to the length measured and sew them to the top and bottom edges of the quilt top. Press the seams toward the blocks.

2. Measure the length of the quilt top through the center, including the just-added borders. Trim two medium tan 1" x 42" strips to the length measured and sew them to the sides of the quilt top. Press the seams toward the blocks.

3. Sew 16 Border Square blocks together end to end. Make two strips. Sew the strips to the top and bottom edges of the quilt top. Sew 18 Border Square blocks together end to end. Make two strips. Sew the strips to the sides of the quilt top.

4. Follow steps 1 and 2 to add the outer border to the quilt top, using the remaining medium tan 1" x 42" strips.

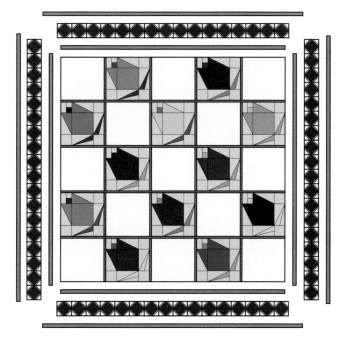

5. Remove the paper foundations.

6. Pin the eight dark brown 1" squares to the quilt top as shown, right sides up. Satin stitch each square in place, using thread that matches the sashing strips.

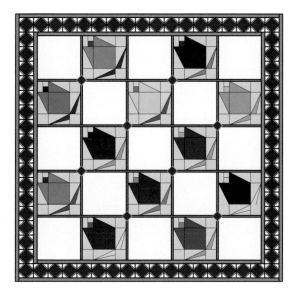

FINISHING THE QUILT

Refer to "Finishing Your Quilt" on pages 17–19 for detailed information on finishing techniques.

1. Piece the quilt backing so that it is approximately 6" longer and 6" wider than the quilt top.

2. Layer the quilt top, batting, and backing; baste the layers together.

3. Hand or machine quilt as desired. This quilt has free-motion feathers going diagonally across the white blocks, and jagged stipple quilting around the flowers. The silky flowers were left unquilted to make them pop out in relief.

4. Bind the quilt with the dark brown strips.

5. Label the quilt and revel in finally getting a second use out of a bridesmaid dress.

What If . . .

→ you used black "tiles" instead of brown for an even sharper contrast?

→ you used only one bridesmaid's dress for the entire quilt, and every flower was the same color?

→ you made the sashing from bridesmaid-dress fabric?

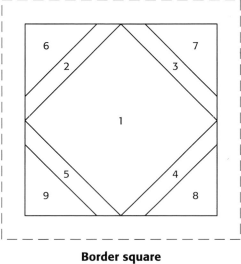

Border square
Paper-piecing pattern

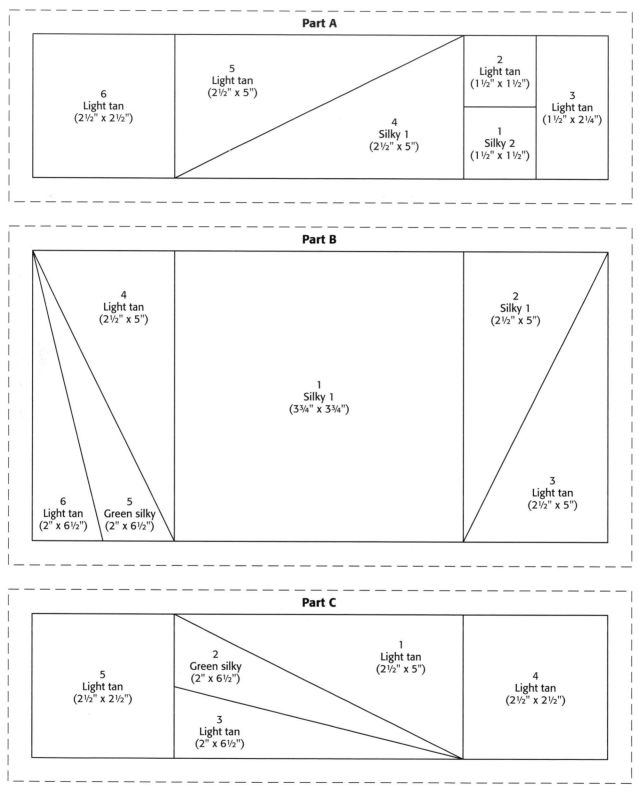

Part A

6
Light tan
(2½" x 2½")

5
Light tan
(2½" x 5")

4
Silky 1
(2½" x 5")

2
Light tan
(1½" x 1½")

1
Silky 2
(1½" x 1½")

3
Light tan
(1½" x 2¼")

Part B

4
Light tan
(2½" x 5")

1
Silky 1
(3¾" x 3¾")

2
Silky 1
(2½" x 5")

3
Light tan
(2½" x 5")

6
Light tan
(2" x 6½")

5
Green silky
(2" x 6½")

Part C

5
Light tan
(2½" x 2½")

2
Green silky
(2" x 6½")

1
Light tan
(2½" x 5")

4
Light tan
(2½" x 2½")

3
Light tan
(2" x 6½")

Tile flower
Paper-piecing patterns

70

Skirting the Issue

Stitched and quilted by Ann Frischkorn.

Finished quilt: 24" x 26" ❖ **Finished block:** 19½" x 21"

The background fabric in this quilt was taken from a skirt that my husband bought me for Christmas the year we got engaged. Three children and 18 years later, the skirt doesn't fit anymore. I was thrilled to drag it from the back of my closet and give it new life. To make the appliqué pieces, I used hand-dyed, felted wool that I purchased online. I love using hand-dyed wool because of its variations of color, which add dimension and richness to any design.

—Ann

MATERIALS

Yardage is based on 42"-wide fabric unless otherwise noted.

1⅛ yards of dark gray felted wool for background and borders

¼ yard of turquoise blue felted wool for flowers and borders

9" x 12" square of terra cotta brown felted wool for urn

6" x 6" square of dark brown felted wool for curlicues

5" x 5" square *each* of 3 different red felted wools for berries

5" x 5" square *each* of 3 different green felted wools for leaves

5" x 5" square *each* of 2 different yellow felted wools for flowers

5" x 5" square *each* of 2 different pink felted wools for flowers

⅜ yard of 100%-cotton fabric for binding

⅞ yard of 100%-cotton fabric for backing

30" x 32" piece of batting

Assorted colors of embroidery floss to match and contrast with felted wool colors

Freezer paper

Chalk marker

Muslin or light-colored fabric, cut to desired size, for a quilt label

CUTTING

All measurements include ¼"seam allowances.

From the dark gray felted wool, cut:

❖ 1 rectangle, 19½" x 21½"

❖ 2 strips, 2½" x 20"

❖ 2 strips, 2½" x 26"

From the turquoise blue felted wool, cut:

❖ 2 strips, ¾" x 19½"

❖ 2 strips, ¾" x 22"

From the 100%-cotton fabric for binding, cut:

❖ 3 strips, 2¼" x 42"

MAKING THE BLOCK

1. Trace patterns A–Q on pages 75 and 76 onto the dull side of freezer paper the number of times indicated. Mark the color on each piece. Cut out each shape about ¼" outside the traced lines. Using a dry iron, press each freezer-paper piece, shiny side down, onto the appropriate color of wool. Cut out each shape on the marked line.

2. Referring to pattern A, use a ruler and chalk marker to transfer the inner detail lines to the urn. Center and pin or staple the urn in place about 2" from the bottom of the dark gray 19½" x 21½" rectangle.

> *Stapling is a great alternative to pinning when you're working with wool. There are no pins to get in your way and it's easy to remove the staples.*

3. Buttonhole stitch the urn in place, using two strands of matching embroidery floss.

Buttonhole stitch.
The smaller the piece, the closer together the stitches should be.

4. Backstitch the detail lines on the urn, using three strands of contrasting embroidery floss.

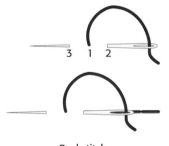

Backstitch

ADDING THE BORDERS

1. Sew the turquoise ¾" x 19½" strips to the top and bottom edges of the rectangle. Press the seams open. Sew the turquoise ¾" x 22" strips to the sides of the quilt top. Press the seams open.

2. Sew the dark gray 2½" x 20" strips to the top and bottom edges of the quilt top. Press the seams open. Sew the dark gray 2½" x 26" strips to the sides of the quilt top. Press the seams open.

Quilt assembly

APPLIQUÉING THE SHAPES

1. Set aside eight E shapes, nine berry shapes (J–O), and three Q shapes for use in the border appliqué. Using the photo on page 71 as a guide, pin or staple the remaining appliqué shapes in place around the urn as desired. Stay about 2" away from the border on all four sides.

2. Use the vine pattern on page 74 to stem stitch the vine in the lower-right corner of the border with three strands of green embroidery floss.

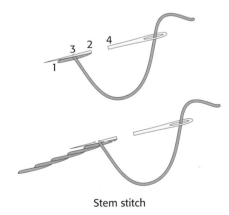

Stem stitch

3. Pin or staple the border appliqué pieces that you set aside in step 1 around the vine.

4. Buttonhole stitch all of the appliqué shapes in place, using two strands of matching embroidery floss.

5. Refer to the patterns to stem stitch the veins in the leaves, the lines in the curlicues, and the lines on the flowers, using three strands of contrasting embroidery floss.

FINISHING THE QUILT

Refer to "Finishing Your Quilt" on pages 17–19 for detailed information on finishing techniques.

1. Cut the quilt backing so that it is approximately 6" longer and 6" wider than the quilt top.

2. Layer the quilt top, batting, and backing; baste the layers together.

3. Hand or machine quilt as desired. The background in this quilt was machine quilted with feathers and a large stipple stitch. The border was quilted with free-form leaves and vines.

4. Bind the quilt with the cotton binding strips.

5. Label the quilt and give new life to old wool.

What If . . .

➤ you used 100% cotton instead of wool?

➤ you used a wool background with silk fabric for the flowers?

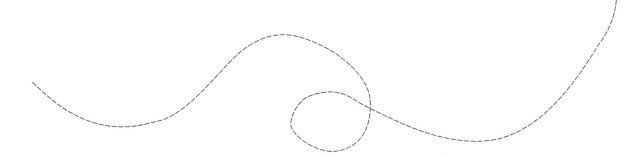

Border vine
Embroidery pattern

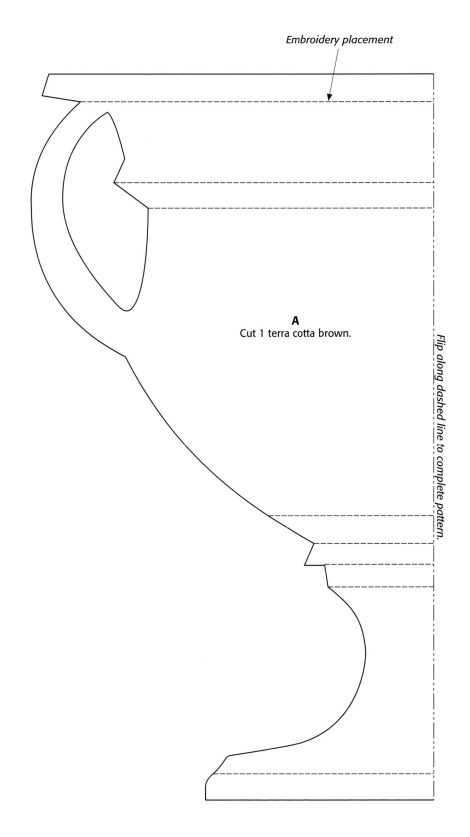

Embroidery placement

A
Cut 1 terra cotta brown.

Flip along dashed line to complete pattern.

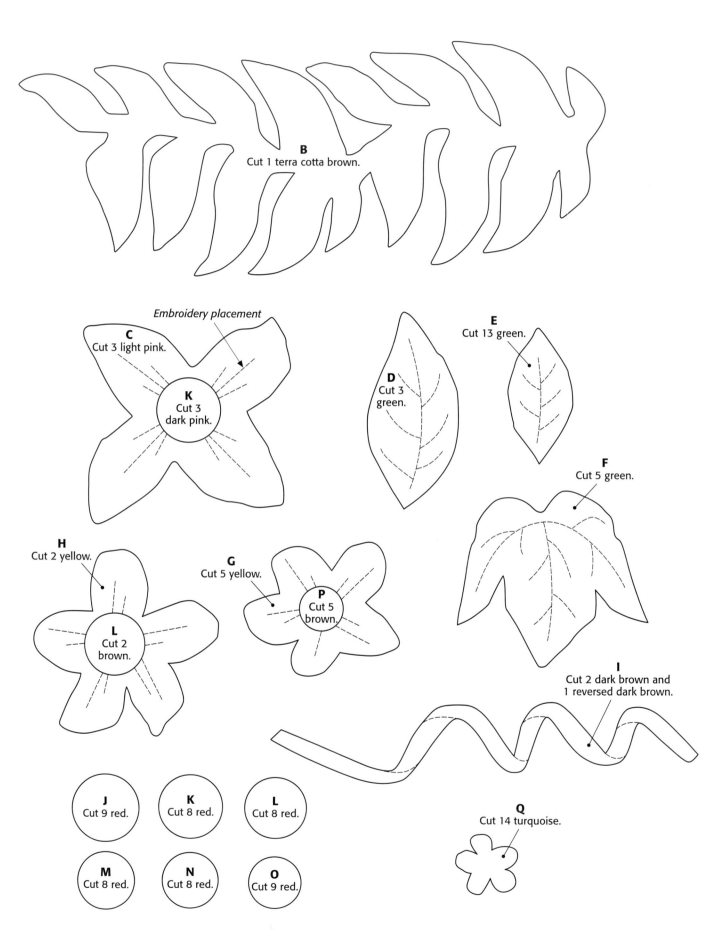

B
Cut 1 terra cotta brown.

Embroidery placement

C
Cut 3 light pink.

K
Cut 3
dark pink.

E
Cut 13 green.

D
Cut 3
green.

F
Cut 5 green.

H
Cut 2 yellow.

G
Cut 5 yellow.

P
Cut 5
brown.

L
Cut 2
brown.

I
Cut 2 dark brown and
1 reversed dark brown.

J
Cut 9 red.

K
Cut 8 red.

L
Cut 8 red.

M
Cut 8 red.

N
Cut 8 red.

O
Cut 9 red.

Q
Cut 14 turquoise.

Resources for Hand-Dyed Wool

Crow Hill Primitives
4 Westvale Rd.
Kennebunkport, ME 04046
www.crowhillprimitives.com
Email: info@crowhillprimitives.com or crow-hill@adelphia.net
Phone: 207-967-0573

Crow Hill has hundreds of colors of hand-dyed wool, and if you still can't find the right shade, send them a swatch of the color you want and they will dye to match.

Homespun Hearth
15954 Jackson Creek Pkwy.
Suite B, #564
Monument, CO 80132
www.homespunhearth.com
Email: customerservice@homespunhearth.com
Phone: 866-346-0414 (toll free)

Moondance Color Company
622 Spencer Rd.
Oakham, MA 01068
www.moondancecolor.com
Phone: 508-882-3383

A Plaid Wool Company
2705 Cantor Dr.
Morgan Hill, CA 95037
www.aplaidwool.com
Email: beth@aplaidwool.com
Phone: 408-776-2999

About the Authors

Ann Frischkorn and Amy Sandrin are quiltmaking partners—and identical twin sisters—who live more than 2,000 miles apart. Ann lives outside of Chicago and Amy lives outside of Seattle. Their quiltmaking journey began when Ann took a beginner's quilting class and knew, after the first stitch, that this was an art form she would embrace for the rest of her life. Not one to miss out on anything, Amy decided to give it a try too. They have been avidly quilting since 1992.

Even though they live far apart, the modern conveniences of digital cameras and email allow Ann and Amy to instantly bounce ideas, color schemes, and design elements off of each other. They have published two other quilting books, one of which is *A Shortcut to Drunkard's Path* (Martingale & Company, 2005). They have been featured on HGTV's *Simply Quilts*, hosted by Alex Anderson, which showcased two different sets of quilting twins.

In their spare time, Ann and Amy collaborate on novels.

New and Bestselling Titles from

Martingale® & COMPANY

America's Best-Loved Craft & Hobby Books®
America's Best-Loved Knitting Books®

America's Best-Loved Quilt Books®

NEW RELEASES

Alphabet Soup
Big Knitting
Big 'n Easy
Courtship Quilts
Crazy Eights
Creating Your Perfect Quilting Space
Crochet from the Heart
Fabulous Flowers
First Crochet
Fun and Funky Crochet
Joined at the Heart
Little Box of Knitted Ponchos and Wraps, The
Little Box of Knitted Throws, The
Merry Christmas Quilts
More Crocheted Aran Sweaters
Party Time!
Perfectly Brilliant Knits
Polka-Dot Kids' Quilts
Quilt Block Bonanza
Quilts from Grandmother's Garden
Raise the Roof
Saturday Sweaters
Save the Scraps
Seeing Stars
Sensational Knitted Socks
Sensational Sashiko
Strip-Pieced Quilts
Tea in the Garden
Treasury of Scrap Quilts, A

Our books are available
at bookstores and your
favorite craft, fabric,
and yarn retailers.
If you don't see
the title you're
looking for, visit us at
www.martingale-pub.com
or contact us at:
1-800-426-3126

International: 1-425-483-3313
Fax: 1-425-486-7596
Email: info@martingale-pub.com

APPLIQUÉ

Appliqué Takes Wing
Easy Appliqué Samplers
Garden Party
Stitch and Split Appliqué
Sunbonnet Sue: All through the Year
WOW! Wool-on-Wool Folk-Art Quilts

LEARNING TO QUILT

101 Fabulous Rotary-Cut Quilts
Happy Endings, Revised Edition
Loving Stitches, Revised Edition
Magic of Quiltmaking, The
Quilter's Quick Reference Guide, The
Sensational Settings, Revised Edition
Your First Quilt Book (or it should be!)

PAPER PIECING

40 Bright and Bold Paper-Pieced Blocks
50 Fabulous Paper-Pieced Stars
300 Paper-Pieced Quilt Blocks
Easy Machine Paper Piecing
Fanciful Quilts to Paper Piece
Hooked on Triangles
Quilter's Ark, A
Show Me How to Paper Piece

QUILTS FOR BABIES & CHILDREN

American Doll Quilts
Even More Quilts for Baby
More Quilts for Baby
Quilts for Baby
Sweet and Simple Baby Quilts

ROTARY CUTTING/SPEED PIECING

40 Fabulous Quick-Cut Quilts
365 Quilt Blocks a Year: Perpetual Calendar
1000 Great Quilt Blocks
Clever Quilts Encore
Endless Stars
Once More around the Block
Square Dance, Revised Edition
Stack a New Deck
Star-Studded Quilts
Strips and Strings

SCRAP QUILTS

More Nickel Quilts
Nickel Quilts
Scrap Frenzy
Successful Scrap Quilts

TOPICS IN QUILTMAKING

Basket Bonanza
Cottage-Style Quilts
Everyday Folk Art
Focus on Florals
Follow the Dots . . . to Dazzling Quilts
Log Cabin Quilts
More Biblical Quilt Blocks
Quilter's Home: Spring, The
Scatter Garden Quilts
Shortcut to Drunkard's Path, A
Strawberry Fair
Summertime Quilts
Tried and True
Warm Up to Wool

CRAFTS

Bag Boutique
Collage Cards
Creating with Paint
Painted Fabric Fun
Purely Primitive
Stamp in Color
Trashformations
Vintage Workshop, The: Gifts for All Occasions
Year of Cats...in Hats!, A

KNITTING & CROCHET

200 Knitted Blocks
365 Knitting Stitches a Year: Perpetual Calendar
Classic Crocheted Vests
Crocheted Socks!
Dazzling Knits
First Knits
Handknit Style
Knitted Throws and More for the Simply Beautiful Home
Knitting with Hand-Dyed Yarns
Little Box of Crocheted Hats and Scarves, The
Little Box of Scarves, The
Little Box of Scarves II, The
Little Box of Sweaters, The
Pleasures of Knitting, The
Pursenalities
Rainbow Knits for Kids
Sarah Dallas Knitting
Ultimate Knitted Tee, The

06/05